I0026843

THE HISTORY OF

TARIFF ADMINISTRATION

IN THE UNITED STATES

From Colonial Times to the McKinley Administrative Bill.

BY

JOHN DEAN GOSS, PH.D.

THE LAWBOOK EXCHANGE, LTD.
Clark, New Jersey

ISBN 9781584775744 (hardcover)
ISBN 9781616190903 (paperback)

Lawbook Exchange edition 2010

The quality of this reprint is equivalent to the quality of the original work.

THE LAWBOOK EXCHANGE, LTD.
33 Terminal Avenue
Clark, New Jersey 07066-1321

*Please see our website for a selection of our other publications
and fine facsimile reprints of classic works of legal history:*
www.lawbookexchange.com

Library of Congress Cataloging-in-Publication Data

Goss, John Dean.
  The history of tariff administration in the United States from
colonial times to the McKinley Administrative Bill / by John Dean
Goss.
     p. cm.
  Originally published: New York : Columbia College, 1891.(Studies
in history, economics, and public law ; v. 1, no. 2).
  Originally presented as the author's dissertation.
  Includes bibliographical references.
  ISBN 1-58477-574-2 (cloth : alk. paper)
  1. Customs administration—United States—History. 2. Tariff—
United States—History. 3. Tariff—Law and legislation--United
States--History. I. Title. II. Series: Studies in history, economics,
and public law ; v. 1, no. 2.
HJ6622.G67 2005
382'.7'0973--dc22   2004057773

Printed in the United States of America on acid-free paper

THE HISTORY OF

TARIFF ADMINISTRATION

IN THE UNITED STATES

From Colonial Times to the McKinley Administrative Bill.

BY

JOHN DEAN GOSS, PH.D.

NEW YORK.

1891.

TABLE OF CONTENTS.

THE HISTORY OF
TARIFF ADMINISTRATION
IN THE UNITED STATES.

INTRODUCTION.

TAXES are necessary for all governments, and the method of their collection has always been the problem of administrators. Let us take it for granted as long since settled that indirect taxation is the best form from an administrative standpoint. Its most frequent and productive application is now found in the taxation of imports. Import taxes, striking the goods in transit, meet them at their weakest point; the machinery of collection can be made simple and accurate in its workings, while the expense of collection may be reduced to a minimum.

Our national government has seen fit (with a few brief exceptions) to confine itself to indirect taxation, and throughout its history has derived the bulk of its revenue from taxes on imports. If the aim of the United States tariff had been exclusively financial, a better knowledge of administrative methods, derived from a study of foreign institutions, an acquaintance with the necessary requirements combined with a developed business ability, would ere now have solved the problem and would have given us a customs administration simple and

(7)

fair, if not—under our present civil service methods—of the highest efficiency and economy. But the adoption of the policy of protection, the very logic of whose honest application compelled the taxation of an almost innumerable list of articles, and the very general introduction of *ad valorem* rates vastly complicated the problem. Another and very difficult element was thus introduced; for the collecting organs, in levying and receiving the tax, not only had to find imported goods and determine their bulk and general nature, but were also compelled to ascertain their value. To do this accurately, for a single class of articles requires an intimate knowledge of its innumerable grades, qualities and textures; an extensive acquaintance with foreign markets, with freight rates, commissions, insurance and a multitude of details imperfectly acquired even by a lifelong business experience. Even in standard articles there remains a wide margin of error; while in the numberless new and rare miscellaneous products that are daily increasing in amount, the assessment of valuation in many cases, must be based upon mere conjecture.

The point of greatest friction in any tax system is obviously that of payment; and the greatest patriotism, the strictest personal and business integrity, have been found insufficient to deter men from deceiving the government in all possible ways. The ideal system is that in which the assessor and the taxpayer are as nearly as possible in hearty accord, and where a fair, open spirit prevails in all their dealings. Not only has the opposite condition of things been firmly established in the United States, but this seems to be the legitimate outcome of any system of *ad valorem* duties. Furthermore, the immense development of the consignment system[1] has brought it about that a vast body of importers, especially in New York—where four-fifths of our imports land—are unnaturalized foreigners, out of sympathy with our institutions, and openly and avowedly using every advantage in their dealings with our government.

---

[1] Finance Report, 1885, Vol. II., p. vi.

As a consequence of these peculiarly embarassing conditions our present customs system has grown to be what it is; and if in its study we find great imperfections or even great injustice, let us in each case remember the manner of its growth—the unhealthy conditions that have fostered these unseemly results. If in its present state we find many things to criticise and some to condemn, let us see whether a brief review of its history will not lead us to conclude that it has been one of progress, auguring well for the future.

CHAPTER I.

THE COLONIAL PERIOD.

THE colonists were farmers, and the farmer of that day was also blacksmith, mechanic, carpenter, cobbler, weaver and jack of all trades. Not only did the colonial farmer hew his own timber, build his own house, make his own furniture, construct his own rude implements, wear home-spun, eat of his own raising and drink of his own brewing; but the few things that he bought came mostly in exchange, and were as limited as were his wants and as simple as were his habits.

Among a people living thus it is small wonder that the revenue from any system of indirect taxation should but barely pay the cost of its collection. Indeed, the result of attempts to enforce the measures by which England sought to gain a revenue from the colonies was usually a net deficit; while the colonies themselves experienced great difficulty in raising money for their own affairs.[1] Direct trade relations with other countries were limited, and in the case of some articles prohibited, by the British Navigation Laws; and though we hear much of a flourishing illicit traffic, we find that the colonial marine was engaged mainly in the fisheries, and that general commerce was small in amount and confined to few articles. Then again we are struck with the simplicity of the laws, the comparative independence of each official, the hatred of restraint and disregard of all rules, that made every officer a mild autocrat and every underling a sturdy insubordinate. As Professor Sumner[2] has so plainly pointed out, the national

[1] Kalb states that after the seven years' war the colonies were all in debt. Life of J. Kalb by Frederick Knapp, p. 291.

[2] Life of Hamilton.

characteristics of the pre-revolutionary and revolutionary times were by no means what we have since come to regard as American.

The revolutionists had unlimited time to talk vaguely on abstract matters of freedom, representation and government; they delighted to get together and discuss their wrongs and rights; but their knowledge of good administrative methods was slight, while their interest in governmental efficiency was not apparent. All their ideas were colored with extravagant notions of individual liberty. It is not strange, therefore, that we find them greatly lacking in administrative ability. They hated system, they hated restraint of any kind, and naturally proved anything but efficient administrative officers.

Various obnoxious English customs acts were passed from time to time, and more or less successful attempts were made to enforce them; but the manner of their enforcement seems to have been left largely to the discretion of the resident English officials, who were far from being exemplary administrators. The whole effect of these laws, instead of instructing the colonists in methods of revenue collection, was to familiarize them with methods of evasion, and to emphasize that almost universal desire to cheat the government, whose presence to-day, even among otherwise honorable people, is such a curious phenomenon in public ethics. Before the adoption of the Constitution, however, nearly all the colonies had imposed slight taxes upon imports. The methods of collection were in most cases prescribed with great looseness if at all; while the agents designated were usually local officers whose functions as collectors of imports were added to, and inextricably confused with, a multitude of other entirely inconsistent duties.

In order to obtain a general survey of the various systems in vogue in the colonies, it will be well to take a chief representative from each system—Virginia for the southern system, Massachusetts for the New England system, New York for the Middle States system. The conditions in these colonies were typical of all the others in the respective classes.

1. Virginia Customs Administration.

One of the earliest colonial customs laws that is recorded, aside from those laws imposing dues upon tonnage, which were almost universal, was that passed by the Council of Virginia in 1657–8.[1] In the compass of some twenty lines it provides for the collection of ten shillings a hogshead on all tobacco raised by the sale of Dutch[2] goods and exported in Dutch vessels; and that any person so required must make statement under oath of all goods brought in or tobacco exported. The commissioner of the county court was required to prevent fraud and to see that the Dutch made truthful statements to the governor's agent under penalty of double the amount involved. Tobacco being practically the sole export of the colony, this was in effect an import tax; but the first strict import duty was not laid till 1661,[3] when rum and sugar were required to pay a certain impost and their unloading was forbidden except at appointed ports.

The primitive mode of collection is indicated by the act of October, 1670, which ordered that duties be paid in " money or good bills of exchange," and not as theretofore in goods; and it appears that at this time the county courts appointed the collectors. In 1691 due entry was required stating the amounts, *etc.*, of dutiable goods on board. The duty was to be paid, or bond given for its payment, before the goods were allowed to be put on shore. In case of false entry a penalty of £100 was imposed for each offense.

No changes of importance took place in the import laws of

---

[1] Henning, Statutes at Large, Vol. I., p. 469.

[2] Dutch was interpreted to mean all foreigners.

[3] The different authors of the Statutes at Large agree in calling this merely a penalty for not unloading at the prescribed places, but the wording of the Statute certainly warrants the statement of the text, which is further confirmed by the quaint heading of the bill—" Whereas excessive abuse of rum hath by experience bin found to bring diseases and death to diverse people and the purchasing thereof made by the exportation and unfurnishing the country of its owne supply and staple articles, be it enacted," *etc.*

this colony until the revolution taxed its strength and compelled it once more to turn to this source for revenue. In October, 1779, "an act for raising a supply of money for the service of the United States" levied a tax of two and a half per cent. *ad valorem* on all goods "imported and bought to be sold again." This curious piece of legislation did not tax goods on their importation, but on their subsequent sale—the tax to be paid by the purchaser; the "vender to render account upon oath to the commissioners of tax" of every such sale exceeding £1000, within one month after it was made, under penalty of triple the duties thereon. These commissioners were empowered to examine every such purchaser on oath as to how much of the goods were "bought to sell again," and how much for his or his family's consumption, and the tax decided to be due thereon was to be collected by the sheriff in the same manner as other taxes. The "venders" of goods at retail were compellable to testify under oath as to the amount of their sales, and to pay an assessment on their stock in trade. Penalties in triple the amount of duties were stipulated throughout the bill, and suits brought to recover penalties had preference over private suits.

It is not surprising that this remarkable enactment was superseded a year later by another act which, in addition to tonnage dues, laid specific duties on wines, liquors, sugar and molasses, and upon "all imported dry goods except salt, munitions of war and iron from Maryland, * * * one per centum upon the value to be ascertained by the cost thereof at the port where laden * * * or put on board by the captain or owner of the vessel importing the same," to be paid in specie at the port of importation by the captain or owner and collected by the "naval officer." In case of non-payment, concealment or delay, the vessel was to be forfeited. A curious provision of this act, and one which puts our colonial legislators in a somewhat ludicrous light, is the clause providing "as an encouragement to captains and masters" to make a true and faithful "return of dutied goods," that they should be allowed to import for each 100 tons burden of their vessel "200 pounds worth of goods at first cost duty free."

In November, 1781, on the recommendation of Congress, that body was empowered by the legislature of Virginia to levy a five per cent. duty, and to appoint collectors and make needful regulations [not repugnant to the state laws and constitution] for the collection of the same. The operation of the act was to be suspended until like action was taken by the other states. Entry was to be made within ten days, and the duty paid in cash, or bond given for six months. The ship master was to pay all duties, and was to be reimbursed by the owner of the goods in case they were imported by a person other than the shipowner. A limited provision was made for what we should call shipment in bond from one county to another; and the usual fines and penalties were prescribed. By this law false entry subjected the wrong doer to a fine of £100, but in May, 1783, this was changed to £200 and forfeiture of the goods so entered. Again in October, 1783, following its recommendations of the preceding April, Congress was empowered to collect certain duties under conditions similar to those of the act of 1781, with the added provision that the Governor was to appoint collectors, who were, however, to be removable by Congress.

It is needless to say that none of these later acts went into effect; the states failing to agree and some absolutely refusing to act at all.

2. Massachusetts Customs Administration.

In Massachusetts, in the earliest times, the collection of imports, like the collection of excises, was farmed out under the supervision of commissioners.[1] The general import tax of November, 1668,[2] was also to be administered by a body of

[1] Numerous references throughout the Records of the Massachusetts Bay Colony. Vol. IV., Pt. II., p. 410; Vol. V., p. 51.

[2] *Ibid.*, Vol. IV., Pt. II., p. 410.

commissioners. The act of the following May[1] (1669) out-
lined the method of collection. Goods were to pay one penny
for every twenty shillings value—this value to be ascertained
by adding twenty per cent. to the value at the place whence
imported. The "master, purser, boateswaine or skipper" of a
ship upon its entering a port and before breaking bulk or landing any goods, must certify their value to the town treasurer
or collector "by him empowered." The collector should thereupon enter in a book kept for that purpose a description of the
goods, their marks and coverings, and the name of the person
to whom sent. Before landing any goods the owner or importer "must signify the true value thereof by showing the
just invoice" to the collector, who should forthwith enter the
gross sum in his books and demand and receive the proper
rates. In case of denial or delay in payment the collector
might levy distress upon the goods. If the invoice were
"falsified, concealed or not produced," the treasurer or collector with the selectmen of each town concerned should rate the
goods "according to their best discretion" at not less than £4
per "tun." In a difficult or doubtful case the officer should
"repair to the governor and council, who would give directions" for the execution of the law.

The order of May 28, 1679,[2] contained additional provisions
requiring all collectors to take oath faithfully to perform their
duties, and providing that no more than the legal fees of two
shillings per pound be exacted. All dutiable goods were to be
landed at appointed wharves, and goods landed without being
entered should be put in a warehouse and secured by the collector until the owner made entry and paid the duties.

In 1692[3] the compensation of the commission appointed by
the governor or council to supervise collection was fixed at
one-sixth of the receipts for their own services and those of

[1] Records of the Massachusetts Bay Colony, Vol. IV., Pt. II., p. 418.
[2] *Ibid.*, Vol. V., p. 214.
[3] June 24, 1692, Acts and Resolves, Vol. I., p. 30.

their under officers; but two years later the commission was abolished, and the matter was given into the control of a single salaried commissioner, who was to appoint the under officers, and with the treasurer to determine their compensation.[1]

This remained the system until the Revolution. The details of the methods of collection were slowly developed, the law being reënacted each year with a few changes and occasional additions down to 1784, the last year in which the regular customs rates for the province were levied. At this time the law required the master of an arriving vessel to make report and deliver a written manifest to the commissioner within forty-eight hours after arrival. He must also take oath that the manifest contained a just and true account of all imported goods,[2] and that he would report any others if discovered. If before this any goods were unladen, the master should forfeit £100.[3] Owners or consignees of goods must make entry of them in writing, " produce an invoice of such goods as pay *ad valorem*," and make oath before the collector in the following form :[4]

"You, A. B., do swear that the entry of goods or merchandize, as by you made, and the value thereof annexed, is *bona fide*, according to your best skill and judgment, according to the price current or the market price of the said goods."

[1] At first the treasurer was also to aid in their appointment.

[2] The law of June 9, 1696, Acts and Resolves, Vol. I., p. 236.

[3] Law of December 7, 1698, Acts and Resolves, Vol. I., p. 348, increased from £50, as required by law of 1697.

[4] The law of June 18, 1697, provided that if the collector suspected the invoice he might compel the importer to make oath to it. In 1717 [June 22, Acts and Resolves, Vol. II., p. 77] all invoices were required to be sworn to, and the subsequent laws contain many forms of oaths. At about this time the " original invoice" was to be exhibited, and where it was suspected that the goods were consigned on foreign account special oaths were required of the person by whom the goods were entered, that he was the real owner, and that no foreigner was in any way interested in the goods. This was rendered necessary by the retaliatory discriminating duties against foreign goods.

If the importer could not produce the invoice of liquors imported by him, the casks should be gauged at his expense and the duties levied thereon accordingly. Twelve per cent, was allowed for leakage,[1] and damage allowance was made on " decayed wines " if claimed within twenty days after entry.[2]

All duties were to be paid before the goods were landed, though the commissioner might at his discretion give limited credits. The master was liable for the duties on all goods listed in his manifest that were not duly entered, and in order to protect himself might retain the goods until they were entered. The ship was also liable for any default of the master or in the payment of duties.[3] The naval officer was not to allow a ship to clear until a certificate was shown him, under the hand of the commissioner, that all duties had been paid. [4] Stores of the ship not to exceed three per cent. of the lading were exempt from entry. The commissioner and his deputies had power to administer oaths and to search for and seize all suspected goods. All penalties, fines and forfeitures recovered were to go one-half " to his majesty for the use of the province " and one-half to the informer.[5] It is interesting to notice that the salary of the commissioner for the year was £60 " for his labor, care and expenses in said office."

3. New York Customs Administration.

The first acts of the Dutch West India Company with reference to the new colony contained provisions for export and import duties. Specific rates were levied on furs and codfish, [6] and among the early ordinances of the Director and the

---

[1] Act of June 24, 1692.

[2] Act of June 9, 1696. Acts and Resolves, Vol. I., p. 236.

[3] Law of December 2, 1698. Acts and Resolves, Vol. I., p. 350.

[4] Law of June 29, 1700. Acts and Resolves, Vol. I., p. 436.

[5] A similar provision is found in the laws of Virginia.

[6] Freedom and Exemptions Granted by the West India Company, June 7, 1629. Laws and Ordinances of New Netherlands, pp. 6-8.

2

Council of New Netherlands, one dated August 19, 1638,[1] required all tobacco exported to be brought to the approved warehouse, inspected by the regular inspector, and the export duty (five out of every one hundred pounds) paid, under penalty of forfeiture of the whole. The ordinance of April 3, 1642,[2] imposed certain export duties and an import duty of ten per cent. "in kind of wares or money" to be paid the "Receiver of the Companies revenues." A little later (1648)[3] all goods were required to be entered with the "Fiscal, or, in his absence at the office of the Receiver," under penalty of forfeiture of the goods and the ship.

Numerous acts followed, the most important being that of April 27, 1656.[4] Under it all goods were to be entered with the farmer of the revenue or his collector, who should attend at the weighing-house on certain hours of certain days therein prescribed. From him, after entry, the "shipper or merchant" would receive a permit of landing, setting forth the full quantity of goods to be unladen, by whom shipped and to whom consigned. The goods should thereupon be "transported"[5] before sundown. Under this ordinance the "Fiscal" was to inspect all departing and arriving vessels. Later provisions[6] forbade goods to be landed till entry had been made and the duties paid. Goods shipped to or from Amsterdam in its trade with this colony were sent through a special warehouse and there opened and marked.[7]

Under the English rule, there was probably at first no great change in the manner of collection, for the law of April 16, 1693, required, as did the former Dutch law, that goods,

---

[1] *Ibid.*, p. 16.   [2] *Ibid.*, p. 31.

[3] *Ibid.*, p. 86.   [4] *Ibid.*, p. 220.

[5] From the context this would appear to mean unladen.

[6] Laws and Ordinances of New Netherlands, p. 350.

[7] Law of 1656, *Ibid.*, p. 245. A peculiar prohibition is to be found among these ordinances, declaring that no person should be allowed to offset against duties due, claims against the Company bought by him from the Company's servants. *Ibid.*, p. 410.

whether exported or imported, be brought to the weigh-house in New York and the duties there determined. By refusal so to do the merchant rendered himself liable to certain forfeitures; in case of successful prosecution therefor, the informer or prosecutor was to get one-half of the sum forfeited, besides his costs.

It is difficult to determine when the different features of the New York system were adopted. In 1720[1] we find that the master, mate or purser of an arriving vessel should repair to the custom house and there "declare all the parcels" of dutiable goods that were on board. The owner or consignee of goods was then to make entry, with the collector or deputy, taking oath that the entry was according to the invoice. In case they were European goods, the entry was to be according to their "prime cost." A copy of the entry being given the treasurer, he should furnish a permit, upon the presentation of which the collector should allow all goods therein designated to be unloaded. At this time six weeks credit was allowed on duties. Twenty years later the system had farther developed, and we find it to be in outline as follows. [2]

The master, mate or purser must within forty-eight hours after the ship's arrival deliver to the treasurer a sworn manifest under his hand, mentioning the quantities of all goods on board and the person to whom they were consigned. The consignee was to make particular entry of the goods, at the same time paying the duties, or, if over ten pounds, securing them to be paid on three months' time. If invoices were produced, he was required to take oath to the effect that the value as stated in the invoice was to the best of his belief the real and true value. If no invoice was produced, the treasurer was to ap-

---

[1] Acts of the Assembly, 1691–1725, Bradford, p. 197.

[2] Law of November 3, 1740. Livingston & Smith, Laws of New York, Vol. I., p. 281. At this time, in addition to various specific duties, all European and East Indian goods imported were to pay five pounds for every one hundred pounds value "prime cost." There was also a duty on slaves imported, and quite extended provisions for its collection.

point " one credible merchant and the importer another, who were to appraise such goods to the best of their judgments," the appraisement to be at the expense of the importer and to settle the real value of the goods.   The certificate of the treasurer as to entry was addressed to the " land and tide waiter "[1]—an inspection officer having supervision of the ship and cargo—and permitted the free landing of the goods. The master must indicate at what wharf he would land them, and if landed at another should forfeit five pounds therefor. If goods were landed without permit they were to be forfeited. Sea stores were to be excepted from the manifest, and ten per cent. allowance might be made for leakage.   Exported goods when reimported after once having paid duty might be admitted free, on oath to that effect being taken and the circumstances indicated.

The next legislation of importance, aside from the conditional laws passed at the request of Congress and which never went into effect, was in 1784[2] when a law of some completeness was enacted, levying specific duties on a considerable list of articles and an *ad valorem* duty of £2 10d on every " £100 value prime cost" on all goods imported excepting some few enunerated, and all goods, wares and merchandise of the growth, product or manufacture of the United States of America or any of them.

The provisions made in this act for collection are of considerable interest, as it seems more than any one other to have formed the basis for the first customs collection laws of the United States.   It provides in outline as follows.

Within seventy-two hours after a vessel's arrival at any harbor in the state (south or east of New York—except Sagg

---

[1] A term borrowed from the English law.   When these officers were first introduced into the New York system does not appear, and their exact duties are no where defined. Section 10 of the law of December 12, 1753, [Van Schaak. Laws of New York, Vol. I., p. 326] requires that they should take an oath not to accept any fee or gratuity whatsoever. See *infra*, law of 1784.

[2] March 22, Laws of New York, Vol. I., p. 599.

Harbor) the master, mate or purser, under penalty of £100 for neglect and £500 for fraud, was to deliver to the collector of the port of New York an exact and true manifest of all " goods, wares and merchandise " which the ship had on board at the time of leaving her last port or subsequently, and particularly specifying the " packages, bales, casks, chests, trunks, cases or boxes " with their marks and numbers, and the names of the owners or consignees. This manifest was to be sworn to according to a prescribed form, and the duties appearing due thereon were to be paid or secured before any goods could be landed. Goods landed in violation of this provision, or at any time between sunset and sunrise, were to be forfeited, and the master was to incur a penalty of double their value. If the collector suspected the manifest he might cause the ship to be thoroughly inspected by the " land and tide waiters," who might affix locks, for further protection, to all hatches, *etc.*, of the vessel during the night.

The next step was for all persons having goods on board to make particular entry of such goods by exhibiting the original invoices, leaving copies of them and taking a prescribed oath as to their accuracy. The duties were ascertained, and if less than £20 were to be paid in cash, or if exceeding that sum were to be secured by a bond with two sufficient sureties on three months' time. Thereupon the collector was to deliver to the importer a certificate directed to any land and tide waiter, stating that the duty on certain goods had been paid or secured and that they might be landed. But in case the collector suspected fraud in the invoice he might cause the goods to be examined, and any packages containing uninvoiced goods were to be forfeited. If any dispute arose as to the value of any dutiable goods, or in case of damage resulting to them on the voyage, appraisement might be had at the expense of the contesting importer. The collector was to appoint one merchant and the importer another, who upon taking oath before a justice of the peace well and truly to appraise the goods, were to determine their value; but in case they were unable to agree they might jointly appoint a third merchant to join them, the decision of any two being binding.

Goods consigned to another state should be so declared in the manifest, and upon fulfilling certain formalities, the person exporting the goods might bring them in duty free, on executing a bond with two sufficient sureties in double the amount of the duty. If within twelve months proof were not produced of the arrival of the goods at their destined port or of their loss at sea, the bond was to be prosecuted. Penalties provided for might be sued in any court of record by any person, one-half to go to the state and one-half to the person bringing suit. The governor, with the consent of the council, was to appoint the collector, gaugers, weigh-masters and land and tide waiters.[1] The collector was to give official bond, to keep books and render quarterly accounts.[2]

On November 18th of the same year, "an act for the establishment of a custom house" was passed, which farther defined the form of official oaths and bonds, the duties and fees of custom officers and provided for the appointment of a "surveyor and searcher," who had practical superintendence of the harbor and of the "land and tide waiters."

In 1786, New York granted to the United States certain imposts enumerated, which were to be collected by the New York officials according to the New York law, their expenses to be deducted from the receipts.[3] On March 12, 1788, the

---

[1] The duties of these officers were prescribed in the law, but are sufficiently indicated by their names.

[2] The pay of the New York collector was "a salary at the rate of £1200 per annum as a full reward and compensation for his services, and for house or office rent, clerk hire, fire-wood, messengers or servants to attend to the office, stationery and all other contingent expenses whatever."

[3] With this style of support, it is little to be wondered at that the Continental Congress was never able to levy an impost duty. This act was to go into effect when the same imposts had been agreed to by the other states—a fine example of New York's dictatorial position.

collector was empowered to appoint certain stores as bonded warehouses, wherein goods might be stored duty free, bonds being given in double the amount of the duties due. The duty was to be paid from time to time as they were withdrawn for use, or remitted in case they were exported within eighteen months after entry.

CHAPTER II.

NATIONAL TARIFF ADMINISTRATION OF THE EIGHTEENTH CENTURY.

UNDER the confederation of 1777 the Continental Congress made numerous but futile efforts to induce the states to join in levying taxes on imports for the benefit of the common treasury.[1] Indeed this was about the only feasible method of raising revenue that the articles would allow. The first or second act passed after the organization of the Congress, under the constitution of 1787, was " an act for laying a duty on goods, wares and merchandise."[2] Besides specific duties on a few articles, this law imposed *ad valorem* duties varying from fifteen to seven per cent. on certain enumerated articles and five per cent. on all other goods, with a few exceptions. In the same month "an act to regulate the collection of duties," *etc.*, was passed.[3] This act divided the country into collection districts, and enumerated the ports of entry and delivery, of which there must be at least one in each district. In some thirty-eight sections it proceeded to form the entire machinery and process of collection. It is plainly a hasty compilation from the laws of the various states—following very closely the late laws of New York, and even copying whole sections almost *verbatim*.

1. Customs Officers.

The collection districts were mapped out then with refer-

---

[1] Rhode Island was the most obstinate in its refusal to comply with the request of Congress, claiming that in some inscrutable way it would tend peculiarly to the detriment of her commerce.

[2] Act of July 4, 1789. Statutes at Large, Vol. I., p. 24.

[3] Act of July 31, 1789. Statutes at Large, Vol. I., p. 29.

ence to the state lines, no district lying in more than one
state; but this has long since been disregarded, and, as the
result of subsequent legislation, district lines now have no
reference to any local divisions.

The officers provided for were the collectors, deputy collectors, naval officers, surveyors, weighers, measurers, gaugers and
inspectors.   Each district was allowed a collector at its port of
entry and a surveyor at each of the ports of delivery.   The
ports of entry also had a surveyor and the larger ones a naval
officer.   Thus the higher officers of what has since become
the normal port were the collector, naval officer and surveyor. [1]
As their duties have in general remained the same, it may be
profitable to notice how they were fixed by this act.

The collector was to receive all reports, manifests and documents, and to keep a record of them, to receive the entry of
all ships and goods together with the invoices of the latter.   He
was to estimate the duties payable thereon and endorse the
same on each entry; to grant all permits of unloading, *etc.*, and
to employ all weighers, measurers, gaugers and inspectors in
addition to such other persons as were necessary.   With the
assent of " the 'principal officer' of the treasury department"
he could designate store-houses for the safe-keeping of goods.

The naval officer[2] was to countersign all orders of the collector, to receive copies of all manifests, and to act in general
as a check upon the collector.

The surveyor was to superintend all weighers, measurers
and gaugers, and to have general supervision of the boarding of
arriving vessels and the inspection of their cargoes.

The deputy collector was appointed by the collector, who
was responsible for his acts, and might exercise the same authority as the collector.

---

[1] Appointed by the President by and with the advice and consent of the Senate.

[2] The usefulness of this officer has been often doubted, and the abolition of
the office altogether strongly urged.

2. *Entry of Goods and Collection of Duties.*

The main provisions of the act and the general method of entry and collection were the same as those previously explained under the New York law of 1784. The master was to deliver two manifests to the boarding officer—one of which was signed and returned to him and the other transmitted to the collector (§ 10). He was also to make entry, under oath, within forty-eight hours after arrival of the vessel, and further entry of goods on board was to be made by the owners. (§ 11).

The inspector took the place of the "land and tide waiter." He had the same functions except that at the expiration of fifteen days[1] from the arrival of the ship he was to take charge of all goods not yet unloaded and hand them over to the collector to be kept for nine months at the risk of the owner in the public stores. If not claimed within that time, they were to be appraised by two reputable merchants and sold for the benefit of the United States.

Ad valorem duties upon all goods at the place of importation should be "estimated by adding twenty per cent. to the actual cost thereof if imported from the Cape of Good Hope or any place beyond the same, and ten per cent on the actual cost if imported from any other place or country, exclusive of all charges" (§ 17). Before permit for landing goods should be given, the duties were to be paid in cash, if under fifty dollars, if more than that sum they might be secured by a bond. The bonds were to run from four to twelve months, according to the class of goods. They were to be signed by one or more sufficient sureties, and in each case of default to be prosecuted by the collector. Ten per cent. discount was allowed for prompt payment (§ 19).

[1] This limit, as found in § 56 of the law of 1799, remained the same until the Act of March 2, 1861, 36 Congress, Sess. II, Ch. 81, where eight days was allowed for a ship under 300 tons, twelve days for one between 300 and 800 tons, and fifteen days for those of over 800 tons.

All drawbacks allowed by law[1] on the exportation of goods, wares and merchandise imported, should be paid or allowed by the collector at whose office the said goods, *etc.*, had been entered and not otherwise, less one per cent. which was retained for the benefit of the United States (§ 31). The bounty allowed on the exportation of fish was to be paid in the same manner.

, If any officer should receive a fee or bribe he should forfeit not less than $200 nor more than $2,000 for each offense, and be forever disabled from holding any office of trust or profit under the United States (§ 35). There was a penalty of not more than $1,000 and imprisonment for not more than one year for false oath of importer or ship master. All penalties, fines and forfeitures were to be divided, one moiety to go to the United States, the other to the collector, naval officer and surveyor of the district, or any one or two of them in the district. But in all cases where there was an informant he should receive the moiety apportioned to the United States (§ 38).

This law remained in force barely one year, and was repealed by the act of August 4, 1790,[2] which was little more than a rearrangement of the one it superseded. This act still more hopelessly jumbled up the officers of the various districts, collectors being assigned to single ports within other collectors' districts, and the whole list being arranged seemingly without any system whatever.

The only additional features of any importance were those regulating the unloading of vessels driven into port by stress of weather and allowing the sale of as much of the cargo as was necessary to pay for repairs. Certain allowances were made for tare, drafts, *etc.*, on bulk goods. Two per cent. was allowed for leakage on wines, *etc.* Damaged goods in both

---

[1] Act of July 4 allowed drawbacks on all articles shipped within twelve months of their entry except on distilled spirits other than brandy or geneva.

[2] Statutes at Large, Vol. I., p. 145, Chap. xxxv.

these acts were appraised in the same manner as goods with a false or defective invoice, or with none at all (§ 35).[1] The President was also authorized to order revenue cutters to be built, officered and armed.

No further changes of importance were made in custom regulations during the next nine years, although the tariff rates were raised and changed at various times. On March 3, 1797,[2] the percentages received by the different officers at the various ports on the gross receipts at their respective points were rearranged and definitely fixed, and the compensations of the lower officers were stated.[3]

3. System Established by Act of 1799.

On March 2, 1799, all former laws were repealed and their place taken by the elaborate enactment which " has remained to this day as the foundation and the framework of subsequent legislation for the taking possession of arriving merchandise and the levying and collecting of duties thereon."[4]

Up to this time the yearly income from customs had never reached ten million dollars,[5] and was far more evenly distributed among the different ports than it has since been. The number of officers at any port was small and the collector had been allowed to use his own common sense and business ability with regard to the direction of office methods and details of the administration, and might please himself as to the forms of most of the documents, bonds, *etc.*, required to pass through his hands. But it was evident that to afford any adequate method of supervision or control, more minute regulations must be imposed and standard forms established. The system had been in operation so long that inspection of

[1] The laws of the colonies had been much more liberal than this, in some the allowance being fixed at as high as twenty per cent.

[2] Statutes at Large, Vol. I., p. 502.

[3] These were increased by act of 1832 and maximum rates fixed.

[4] Secretary Manning in Finance Report for 1885, Vol. II., p. iv.

[5] In 1800 it was $9,080,932.

accumulated records and comparison of forms and methods
followed in the light of the experience which their operation
had given, could furnish an ample basis on which to construct
a more complete working system—a codification, as it were,
of customs administrative law. This Congress proceeded to
do, and with such remarkable skill and thoroughness that,
although our revenues from imports have doubled many times
over since then, and in spite of the bewildering complexity
and variety of articles subject to duty as well as of the im-
proved means of transportation and the many changes in the
facilities and methods of conducting business, the act passed
in 1799 has remained the trunk upon which all subsequent
enactments have been grafted. It fills eighty-two pages in the
statute book and goes into great detail, containing no less
than fifty-six forms, prescribing eleven different bonds, indicat-
ing fourteen different kinds of schedules and providing for
nineteen separate oaths.

The system provided for local agencies with the collectors
at their head. The collector was the agent for communica-
tion with the other departments and with the central authorities. In the larger ports his more important acts were
supervised by a naval officer, and his chief lieutenant out of
doors was the surveyor. The duties of the minor officers were
more or less minutely defined and were in general as previously described. The country was again redistricted, this
time on a definite plan, with one port of entry in each district
at which the collector of the district resided. There might
also be a surveyor, and possibly a naval officer, according to
the importance of the district. Other ports of delivery of sufficient importance within the district were provided with surveyors. The principal officers were required to give bonds, and
all officers were required to take oath that they would faithfully
perform their duties. This was taken before any competent
magistrate by the collector, and before the collector by all the
other officers, and was then to be transmitted to the comp-
troller.

The provisions for the delivery of the manifest, its contents and form were exactly prescribed, but followed in general the provisions of the previous laws, except that special formalities and papers were required for cargoes containing spirits, wines or teas. Special bonds were required for shipment from district to district or to a foreign port. The manifest was now required to contain a list of all passengers and a description of all their baggage, together with a complete account of all remaining "sea stores" and ship supplies, which of course were to be exempt from duty.

"Wearing apparel, and other personal property, and the tools and implements of a mechanical trade only," belonging to persons who arrived in the United States, were free and exempted from duty (§ 40).[1] Descriptions of all baggage and its contents were required to be furnished, and an oath taken that they were intended solely for the use of the person importing or for the use of his family. But in lieu of the latter declaration the collector and naval officer, whenever they saw fit, might cause the baggage to be searched and duty levied on all goods found therein, which in their opinion ought not to be exempted. In case any articles were found which were not enumerated in the entry, they were to be forfeited and the person in whose baggage they were found was to forfeit treble their value. Entry of goods by owner, agent or importer was to be made within fifteen days after the master's report, and the formalities therefor were fully described. As in the former laws, the collector was still permitted at his discretion to hold so much of the goods as he deemed sufficient to secure the duties, in place of sureties on the bond; and in case of default on the bond he might sell them at public auction, rendering the overplus to the importer.

The duties of the various officers were more accurately mapped out than in the former acts; the forms of their certifi-

---

[1] For the present provisions see "Wearing apparel," Free List § 2 of the last act.

cates to importers and their reports to the collector were prescribed, and the previous set of fines and penalties was left practically unaltered.

Over ten pages were filled with regulations respecting the
exportation of goods on which drawback was allowed. In
substance they required the exporter of imported goods entitled to drawback to show within one year after exportation if
to Europe, or two years if to Asia, a certificate from the foreign
consignee, receipting for and declaring to have received the
goods, which were specifically described; this to be sworn to by
the chief officer of the vessel bearing the goods and to be confirmed by a certificate under the hand and seal of the consul or
agent of the United States residing at such place, stating the
same to be true or to be " worthy of full faith and credit."
Where there was no resident consul or agent the certificate of
the consignee was to be supported by that of two " reputable
American merchants residing at said place, or, if there were no
such American merchants, by the certificate of two reputable
foreign merchants." This clause is of interest as being the
first mention of consular participation in the verification of invoices, and as probably suggesting the subsequent extension
of this practice to imported goods also,[1] which has since become a prominent feature and one of the greatest sources of
annoyance and scandal in our entire revenue system.

All officers of customs were forbidden under penalty of five
hundred dollars to be concerned directly or indirectly in ship-
ping or commerce. The act also repeats the " moiety provisions " of the old law with regard to the division of moneys
received from fines and forfeitures, with the addition that when
the information was contributed by any officer of a revenue
cutter, one-quarter should go to the United States, one-quarter
to the customs officers, and the remainder be divided among
the officers of the cutter " agreeably to their pay."

It was further provided that, except in certain districts, no

[1] Act of April 20, 1818.

goods were to be brought into the United States except by sea and in vessels of at least thirty tons burden (§ 92). " Useful beasts " imported for breeding puposes, upon oath or affirmation to that effect, were allowed to be brought in free. One section (§ 102), provided that cutters and boats used in the revenue service " shall be distinguished by an ensign and pendant [sic] with such marks thereon as shall be directed by the President." [1]

The minimum size of casks and packages in which beer, wine, *etc.*, should be imported was prescribed (§ 103). This is the forerunner of that vexatious legislation restricting the size and shape of imported packages; the cause of no little grumbling under our most recent tariffs. The remaining sections of the bill provided for the transportation of Canadian goods through our territory in bond, the goods being subject to entry and examination in the same way as goods imported for consumption.

On the same day another and supplemental statute was passed fixing the rates of fees, the division of them among the various officers, and the compensation of the minor persons in the service.

[1] The revenue flag was adopted and announced in the circular of the Secretary of the Treasury, Aug. 1, 1799.

CHAPTER III.

THE DEVELOPMENT OF THE SYSTEM ESTABLISHED BY THE ACT OF 1799 UP TO THE CIVIL WAR.

1. Prevention of Undervaluation.

AFTER the passage of the exhaustive Act of 1799 very little tinkering was done with customs administration for a number of years.[1] From time to time minor regulations of little importance were imposed, and special temporary measures were adopted during the war of 1812. In 1816 the pay of all the minor officers was increased one-half. On March 3, 1817,[2] the rule regulating the estimation of values on goods subject to *ad valorem* rates was changed so as to read " it shall be calculated on the net cost of the article at the place whence imported, exclusive of packages, commissions, charges of transportation, export duty and all other charges," with the usual additions theretofore established of twenty per cent and ten per cent. respectively.

The next important act after that of 1799 was that of April 20, 1818, whereby the time for which goods were to be held, when not admitted to entry because of the failure of importer to produce the original invoice, was shortened to six months (nine months if from beyond the Cape of Good Hope).[3] And

---

[1] List of intervening Acts: March 2, 1803, Statutes at Large, Vol. II., p. 209; February 22, 1805, Statutes at Large, Vol. II., p. 315; April 21, 1806, Statutes at Large, Vol. II., p. 399; February 4, 1815, Statutes at Large, Vol. III., p. 196; March 3, 1815, Statutes at Large, Vol. III., p. 231.

[2] Statutes at Large, Vol. III., p. 369.

[3] Former laws had required the original invoice to be produced, but no special method of procedure in default thereof was established. The method probably followed was that prescribed where goods were not entered within the fifteen days allowed. *Cf. supra*, p. 26.

3 (33)

the Secretary of the Treasury was given the authority, if he deemed it expedient, to direct the collector to admit the goods to entry *on an appraisement.* The President was to appoint two persons well qualified to perform that duty, at a salary of $1,500 per annum (at New York $2,000), to be appraisers at each of the ports of Boston, New York, Philadelphia, Baltimore, Charleston and New Orleans. On taking oath " faithfully to inspect and examine " goods, and to " report the true value thereof when purchased " to the collector, these persons, together with a disinterested resident merchant selected by the importer, were to act as a board of appraisement where appraisement should be required and directed (§ 9).[1] The collector might direct such appraisement whenever, in his opinion, " there shall be just grounds to suspect that goods, wares and merchandise * * * * have been invoiced below the true value " (§ 11). If the appraised value exceeded that declared in the invoice by twenty-five per cent., then in addition to the regular ten or twenty per cent., there should be added fifty per cent. on the appraised value. On this aggregate amount the duties should be estimated.[2]

Prior to this time it had been customary for the collector to accept the invoice accompanied by the oath of the person making entry, as exhibiting the real dutiable value of the goods imported. But the greatly increased duties imposed in 1816 had proved too strong a strain on the consciences of many importers; and the conviction had forced itself upon observant persons that undervaluation was frequently resorted to. This legislation was thus adopted as a protection to the revenue and to the honest importer.

[1] When appraisement was to be made in ports other than those above named, two respectable resident merchants selected by the collector, together with one chosen by the party in interest, were to constitute the board.

[2] In all cases where the value thus appraised exceeded the invoice value by less than twenty-five per cent., the appraised value was to be taken as the true one. But wherever the invoice value exceeded the appraised value, the former was to govern in the same manner as if no appraisement had been made.

As a further protection against undervaluations it was provided that in addition to the oath required of the owner, importer, consignee or agent on the entry of any goods, wares or merchandise,[1] such owner, consignee, agent or importer should declare on oath, when goods were entered subject to an *ad valorem* duty, that the invoice produced by him "exhibits the true value of such goods, wares or merchandise in their actual state of manufacture, at the place from which the same were imported." In case of consignment if the person authorized to receive them did not appear to make this oath, the goods were to be stored at the owner's risk in the public warehouse. And if the oath was not made or produced within four months, the goods were to be subject to appraisement.

It was also provided (§ 8) that goods imported and belonging to a person residing, at the time being, outside of the United States, should not be admitted to entry unless the invoice of the goods was verified in the manner prescribed (in the 5th section) before the consul of the United States at the port from which the goods were shipped, or before a consul of the United States in the country in which that port was situated.[2] He should further declare on oath as to whether he was in any way interested in the profits of their manufacture, and if so that the prices charged in the invoice represented the current value at the place of manufacture and such as he "would have received if the same had been there sold in the usual course of trade."

By this law the value of goods subject to *ad valorem* rates was to be estimated by including all charges except commissions, outside packages and insurance. As an additional precaution against fraud in the invoice, the collector was required to cause at least one package of every invoice and one package at least out of every fifty packages to be opened and examined. If this package was found not to correspond with, or to be

---

[1] That required by the law of 1799.

[2] If there were no consul in the country, the oath could be taken before a notary public or other officer authorized to administer oaths.

falsely charged in, the invoice, full examination of all goods contained in the invoice was to be made. If any package were found to contain goods not described in the invoice, the whole of that package was to be forfeited and an appraisement of all the goods was to be taken, as prescribed in section eleven.

Undoubtedly, as has often been claimed, frauds of some magnitude have been successfully perpetrated by collusion in the designation of the packages to be examined, as required by this section and its subsequent modifications. But as no good remedy except the cumbersome and expensive one of examining all goods and packages has so far been proposed, and as this only demands for its honest enforcement that the officers be reasonably honest, we must really charge the frauds not to defective regulations but to dishonest service. It may be as well to state what we must always keep in mind in dealing with any method of tax collection; namely: that, while avoiding the introduction of undue temptations in any form and restricting as far as possible all opportunities for collusion, we must proceed on the assumption that the public servants are honorable. It is utterly and plainly impossible to do any work well with rotten machinery.

During the years from 1818 to 1823, and more particularly in 1820, there arose in connection with the proposed increase in protective duties an active agitation for "reforms" and changes in the administration of customs revenue. Resolutions were introduced in Congress in December, 1819, for the abolition of drawbacks,[1] and bills were framed providing for a considerable shortening of what seem to us the unreasonably long credits then allowed on importations. But the proposals met with such a storm of opposition and with such an overwhelming mass of arguments for the retention of the old system that nothing came of them, and the matter rested for ten years.[2] Connected with this was the more successful outcry against the so-called "auction system."

[1] *Cf. supra*, pp. 27 and 31, and *infra*, p. 84.
[2] See article in *North American Review*, Vol. XII., p. 60.

2. *The Auction System.*

Whether the auction system was really a serious affliction to American merchants, we cannot strictly say.[1] It would seem that there would have been many other ways open for the accomplishment of the same results, had there been no such thing as the " auction system." But rightly or wrongly the merchants, oppressed by the hard times and " low prices " of that period, seeking for some cause or some unfortunate institution on which to vent their spite, pounced upon this system, bitterly attacked it and made it the scape-goat of all their misfortunes.[2] It was really a combination of circumstances that made it prominent. But it was the loose methods of the custom house, and the inadequate protection against fraudulent undervaluation, together with the high duties of the tariff of 1816 that rendered it oppressive; or we should rather say that it was these latter facts which formed the true oppression to the honest American importer, and not the much abused " system " which happened to be the final and most conspicuous, although really most innocent, part of a line of fraud that ran back through the custom house and had its impulse in the dull times and over-production in Europe.

The stagnation in business in the years immediately following the last Napoleonic war was marked. The extravagant hopes of great commercial activity upon the renewal of the long-suspended trade relations, and the re-opening of the continental markets, caused an immense production of goods in

[1] *Cf.* Essay on the Warehousing System and the Government Credits, published by the Philadelphia Board of Trade, 1828, p. 18.

[2] The auction system was very widespread and was prominent for many years. But as a cause for tariff evasion it may be easily overestimated. Indeed we have practically the same system of consignment to-day without any general use of the auction room. In this connection undue prominence is given the auction system by some writers. Bolles, in his " Financial History of the United States," finding a temptingly large literature on the subject, has utilized it to fill a considerable part of the space which he devotes to the discussion of customs collection. It is perhaps unnecessary to warn the reader against placing implicit confidence in Mr. Bolles' work.

England, which impoverished Europe was unable to purchase. The great accumulated stocks of British manufacturers, in most cases produced on credit, necessitated the forcing of a market somewhere and at any price.   Facilities were found for this, it is claimed, ready at hand in the auction system so prevalent at that time.

Foreigners would ship in their goods, the auctioneer giving the custom-house bonds, since it was necessary that these bonds be given by a citizen of the United States.   As the goods were greatly undervalued in the invoice, and were immediately sold for what they would bring, there was very little expense in the transaction.[1]   Opposition raged for years against the system, and New York finally levied a tax upon auction sales.[2]

Of course the only remedy for these frauds was found in the deterrent legislation which commenced in 1818, and which was further perfected by the Act of March 1, 1823.   This drew a plain distinction between goods purchased abroad to be imported by the purchaser, and those not actually acquired by bargain or sale, but imported by the manufacturer.

This legislation set out at length the forms of entry and the oaths to be administered by the collector.   They were all very full and explicit, and apparently left no room for quibbling or deceit without perjury.

1st. The consignee, importer or agent, was to swear in substance that the invoice presented was the only one received, expected or known to exist; that it was unaltered; that nothing was concealed to the disadvantage of the United States; that on receipt of any other invoice it would be made known to the collector; and that to the best of his knowledge and belief the invoice produced exhibited the actual cost or the fair

---

[1] The total receipts from such sales between 1810 and 1828 are estimated at $225,000,000.

[2] See Remarks on the Auction System as practiced in New York (N. Y., 1828.). Memorial presented to Congress by the citizens of Philadelphia, Feb., 1817, and Memorial from the State of Delaware; in the Addresses of the Philadelphia Society for the Promotion of Industry, pp. 265 and 274.

market value of the said goods, *etc.*, "at the time or times and place or places where procured or purchased," and no other or different "discount, bounty or drawback, but such as has been actually allowed on the same."

2d. The owner's and purchaser's oath was very much the same as the foregoing with the added clause, that the invoice contained a "just and faithful account of the actual cost of said goods, and of all charges thereon, including charges of purchasing, carriage, bleaching, dyeing, dressing, finishing, putting up and packing."

3d. The manufacturer's and owner's oath was the same as the second, except that in place of the words "actual cost," are substituted: "a just and true valuation of the goods at their fair market value."

Section seven repeated in slightly changed form the requirement[1] of authentication by a United States consul or commercial agent or a public officer. In case of the absence of such authentication, the goods were to be deemed suspected and liable to the same additions and penalties as in case of fraudulent invoices.

Practically the same regulations as to appraisement were retained, but with the addition (§ 18) that in all cases where the owner, consignee, importer or agent was dissatisfied with the appraisement it would be lawful for him to employ, at his own expense, two respectable resident merchants who, after being duly qualified, should act with the two official appraisers as a board of appraisement, and should report the value of the goods if they agreed therein and, if not, the circumstances of their disagreement, to the collector. If the importer were still dissatisfied he might appeal the case to the Secretary of the Treasury who was fully empowered to decide thereon. One-half the excess of duties, caused by adding fifty per cent. in case the reappraisement raised the invoice more than twenty-five per cent., was to be divided, according to the

[1] § 8, see *supra*, p. 35.

moieties clause of the act of 1799, except that in no case should the appraisers be entitled to receive any part thereof. Under this act dutiable value was estimated by including all charges except insurance. But the appraisers were to value goods at the "current value at the time of exportation in the country where the same may have been originally manufactured or produced."

3. Appraisement Reforms of 1830.

Although these laws must have been a check to the grosser frauds upon the revenue, the importer's invoice was still received in the majority of cases as correct, and no examination or appraisement was ordered unless the suspicions of the collector happened to be aroused. It was becoming evident, however, that a scheme of valuation which relied so completely on the honesty of none too scrupulous foreign importers was a direct discrimination against native dealers, and placed too high a premium upon perjury, with too slight means for its detection to work at all justly.

The tariff law of May 19th, 1828,[1] declared that in all cases where *ad valorem* rates were levied upon goods imported, it should be the duty of the collector to have them appraised at their actual value, "any invoice or affidavit thereto, to the contrary notwithstanding," and that in all cases where the actual value so ascertained should exceed the invoice value by ten per cent., fifty per cent. additional should be charged; that is, the duties should be raised one-half. The stringency of this provision, however, was greatly lessened by a proviso that nothing in the section should be construed to impose this fifty per cent. additional for a variance of a *bona fide* invoice of goods from their actual value.

About this time the general discussion of the tariff and the continued prominence of tariff questions in the public mind seems to have called some attention to the methods of its administration as well.

[1] Statutes at Large, Vol. IV., p. 274.

No better opportunity could be offered for a change in methods than that which a change of principles affords. When the people begin to distrust an old principle, they are apt to distrust all things connected with it. When they attempt to discard a settled policy, they are willing to throw off with it many of the purely incidental features of its application. They are then open to reforms, changes, even experiments. That there was need of reform in the customs administration was plainly evident in many directions. A mere examination of the records of some departments is sufficient to condemn them. As a sample of the inefficiency of parts of the service and the general laxness in the system of public accounts prevalent at this time, it is only necessary to state that during the seven years preceding 1828 the nominal exports of spices on which drawbacks were obtained, in spite of the fact that they were not produced, but, on the contrary, were extensively consumed in the United States, exceeded the nominal imports by $168,155. As further illustrative of the condition of the service under the method of compensation in large part through fees,[1] it may be mentioned that in many places the inspectors received more than double the compensation of the collectors who employed them.[2] Great embarrassment in the conduct of business was also experienced by the various ways in which these fees were computed. There was hopeless lack of order in the classification of the various ports. At some the custom houses were built or purchased by the government; while at others the collectors were compelled to furnish them at their own expense.

The report of the Secretary of the Treasury for 1829 called the attention of Congress to some of the objectionable features of the prevailing practice, and indicated certain necessary reforms which Congress partially incorporated in the law of May 28, 1830.

---

[1] See repealing laws of 1870 and 1890, *infra*, pp. 68 and 87.

[2] Report of Secretary Ingham, December, 1829.

The President was authorized to appoint an additional appraiser for New York,[1] and the Secretary of the Treasury to
appoint not exceeding four *assistant appraisers,* two in Philadelphia and two in Boston,[2] "who shall be practically acquainted with the quality and value of some one or more of
the chief articles of importation." They were to examine such
goods as the principal appraisers might direct, and report the
value to them for revision and correction before it was handed
to the collector. But in any case where the collector deemed
the appraisement too low he might direct a reappraisement,
either by the principal appraisers or by three merchants designated by him for that purpose. If the importer was dissatisfied with the appraised value, he should apply to the collector
in writing, stating the reasons for his opinion. Thereupon the
collector was to appoint one merchant " skilled in the value of
such goods," and the merchant was to appoint another. In
case of disagreement, these two were to appoint an umpire.
When a majority of them agreed, they should report the result
to the collector. In case this differed from the value set by
the government appraisers, the collector was to decide between
them. One package at least out of every twenty was now to
be examined.[3]

A provision which was the forerunner of several similar
ones that have caused great annoyance to appraising officers
was the one requiring that when goods of which cotton or
wool was a component part were found in the same package,
the value of the best article contained in such package should
be taken as the average value of the whole. Indeed as the law
went promptly into effect there was very general complaint

---

[1] Heretofore two appraisers had constituted the force at New York, but the law
of 1828, requiring the appraisement of all goods imported, threw an overwhelming amount of work upon them, as at this time more than half the total imports
entered at that port.

[2] Their salaries were to be at New York $1500 a year; at Philadelphia and
Boston $1200.

[3] Formerly one in fifty. See *supra,* p. 35.

from importers, who from the lack of sufficient notice were compelled in some instances to pay unreasonable duties. There was no definite requirement as to what size and form of parcel should constitute a package, and some kinds of goods such as laces, *etc.*, were, it was claimed, almost necessarily imported in packages containing several classes of different values. This affords an illustration of what complications a seemingly simple provision may create.

In his report for 1830 Secretary of the Treasury Ingham made several suggestions looking to changes in revenue collection in contemplation of expected tariff legislation. By far the most important of these was the substitution of "home valuation" in place of the "foreign valuation," which had always hitherto been the basis of appraisement. In the course of a somewhat extensive argument, he called attention to the impossibility of the officers keeping themselves informed as to current value in foreign markets with sufficient precision to render it an item of uniform ratio to that of current value in the United States.

This same difficulty exists to-day. But he went on to show that as long as the current value, or rather the invoice price of goods in the foreign market, was made the basis on which duties were laid, peculiar advantages were given to those having special opportunities of purchasing or making up invoices at rates below the real value; that is, advantage was given to the foreign merchant who thereby had the benefit not only of greater intimacy with the foreign markets—which might be presumed to be offset by the American's advantage in selling —but also of the fact that he could in consequence enter his goods lower and pay less duties. It was chiefly owing to this that extensive branches of importing business were tending to fall more and more into the hands of foreign merchants, and of those who, whether foreign or American, were least scrupulous in their dealings. Subsequent experience has borne out . these statements. But they seem to be the inherent tendencies of any *ad valorem* system, if not its necessary results. The remedy proposed was to adopt " the current value in the United States " as the dutiable value—disregarding, of course, the cost in the foreign market, and excluding all charges and additions. It was urged in support of this plan that the officers, by proper attention and diligence, could readily ascertain the current value of goods in their vicinity, that a mass of information could speedily be collected to correct errors, and that the effect of such an arrangement would be to steady prices, to expose merchants to less hazard, and to restore as far as possible the equality between foreign and domestic dealers.

This principle was adopted in the law of March 2, 1833, but its application was to be postponed till after June 30, 1842.[1] Before that time had arrived, a secretary hostile to the plan had taken office, and the great difficulties of its enforcement were more plainly seen, so that it was in actual or rather attempted operation for only a few months before its repeal, in 1842.[2] Several years later, during Pierce's administration, the idea was again taken up, but was handled so roughly by Guthrie,[3] then Secretary of the Treasury, that it was abandoned, and the experiment has never since been attempted.

The change in the tariff in 1832 brought with it some additional regulations.

The Act of July 14, 1832, which was not to go into effect until the third of the following March, abolished the long standing custom of adding ten per cent. or twenty per cent. to the cost or value of goods in estimating the duty thereon. Duty less than two hundred dollars[4] was to be paid in cash without a discount; if it exceeded that sum it might be paid or secured to be paid one-half in three and one-half in six

---

[1] House Report, No. 943. 27th Congress, 2d Session.

[2] Bolles in his Financial History makes a misstatement here. *Cf. supra*, p. 37, note.

[3] Report of Secretary of Treasury, 1856.

[4] The law had heretofore placed fifty dollars as the limit.

months,[1] an exception being made in case of woolen goods. [2] This was a very much needed reform, as the terms of credit had heretofore varied greatly on different classes of goods, thus without any reason favoring some imports much more than others and resulting in manifold useless and expensive complications. The time allowed on bonds had, up to this time, varied all the way from three months to two years, according to the nature of the merchandise and the country whence it was imported.[3] These changes, which on the whole considerably shortened credits, aroused, as was natural, a great deal of opposition among importers.

This same law (§ 8) made it lawful for the appraisers to summon any person and examine him on any matter which they deemed relevant to the determination of the value of any merchandise imported, to require him to produce any letters, accounts or invoices relating to the same; and if the person so required should fail to attend or refuse to answer, he was subject to a fine of fifty dollars. In case he was the owner the appraisement was to be final. The duty was imposed upon the Secretary of the Treasury, of establishing such rules and regulations not inconsistent with the laws, as the President

---

[1] Section 27 of the law of March 1, 1823, provided that where the duty was paid in cash a discount was to be allowed at the rate of four per cent. per annum, for the legal term of credit allowed on those duties.

[2] See *infra*, pp. 50–51.

[3] The terms had been for duties on the produce of the West Indies (except salt), or of places north of the equator and situated on the eastern shores of America, one-half in six months and one-half in nine months; on salt nine months; on wines twelve months: on all goods imported from Europe (other than salt, wines and teas); one-third in eight months, one-third in ten months, and one-third in twelve months: on all goods (other than salt, wines and teas), imported from places other than Europe and the West Indies, one-third in eight months, one-third in twelve months, and one-third in eighteen months: on teas, stored as security two years, when delivered for consumption, the duties not less than $100 in four months; between $100 and $500 in eight months; over $500 in twelve months; but not in any case to extend beyond the two years allowed: on wines and spirits stored for delivery, the same credit on delivery as if not stored, not to exceed twelve months.

should think proper to secure "a just, faithful and impartial appraisal of all goods." This provision placed in the revised statutes (§ 2949), remains to-day the basis for the Secretary's regulations.

By this same act (March 2, 1833) the jurisdiction of the circuit courts of the United States was extended to all cases in law or equity arising under the revenue laws of the United States, for which other provisions had not already been made by law; and when any action was commenced in a state court against any government officer or other person for or on account of any act done under the revenue laws, such action might be removed to the circuit court on petition of the defendant. The necessity of this provision is plainly evident, and it is strange that it was not sooner enacted.

4. Payment of Duties in Cash.

In the frequent changes of the tariff during these years of agitation it was noticed that owing to the terms of credit allowed on all imports the direct effect of any change in rates was not felt at once in the revenues; but the government was forced to wait till the maturing of the bonds given on the importations under any new schedule. It was thus utterly impossible for the government to meet promptly any sudden demand for increased revenues. The effect of any law was postponed and obscured, so that its real result could not be immediately or even eventually determined with accuracy. It was thought necessary to adopt some system whereby the public income could be made to respond more quickly to public enactments.

To accomplish this a law of this same date, (March 2, 1833,) provided that all duties should be paid in ready money; but like all the tariff laws of this period, it was a compromise, and was not to take effect until after June 30, 1842.

In support of this provision, the similar practice of European nations was cited, and it was claimed, and with considerable basis of fact, that the credit system fostered dangerous speculation which not only was injurious to the people, but jeopardized the revenue.[1] It would have been far more advantageous for the government had this law been allowed to go into immediate operation. For many importers failed in the crash of 1837, and through the non-payment of their bonds in connection with the suspension of importation resulting from the hard times the government found itself in sore need of money. Indeed, the great fault in the credit system was not that it delayed the receipt of the revenue,—the warehousing system does that,—nor that it so greatly fostered speculation—for that was due mainly to other causes,—but that it endangered the revenue by compelling the government to accept inadequate security, and gave the importers credit from the government, which should have been sought from individuals. It is a rather remarkable testimony to the honesty of importers, that up to 1830, of the $781,000,000 to that time secured for duties under the old credit system, the whole loss was less than $6,000,-000.[2]

5. The "Similitude Section" and the Warehouse System.

The next important tariff act was that of August 30, 1842, which in its treatment of collection problems was somewhat reactionary, as a result probably of a change in administrations and of secretaries. It reimposed the old ten per cent. discrimination against goods imported from beyond the Cape of Good Hope, but with the added clause, "in foreign vessels." The dutiable valuation (§ 16) was fixed as the "market value or wholesale price" of the goods "at the time when purchased in the principal markets of the country from which the same shall have been imported," to which should be added all costs

[1] Essay on the Warehousing System and the Government Credits, Phila., 1828. We must remember in estimating the effect of credits, that this was a time of widespread speculation in all lines, as a result of the changed financial policy of this country, and it may be doubted whether it was any more prevalent in the importing business than in most others.

[2] See Finance Report for 1831, Vol. III., p. 235.

and charges except insurance and including in every case a charge for commissions at the usual rates. Unfinished goods were to be taken and estimated as of the same value as they would have been if entirely finished at the time when purchased and at the place whence imported.

Where the importer was dissatisfied with the appraisement, upon notice given forthwith in writing of such dissatisfaction the collector should appoint two " discreet and experienced merchants, residents of the United States, and familiar with the character and value of the goods in question" to examine and appraise the same. If they should disagree "the collector should decide between them,"[1] and the appraisement should be taken as final.

The provision of the former law, imposing a fine of fifty per cent. if the appraised value exceeded the invoiced value by ten per cent. or more, was reënacted with the omission of the former exception in case the invoice were *bona fide*, and the addition of a fine of five thousand dollars for each false invoice. The collector was required to designate at least one package out of every ten to be opened and examined, thus increasing the requirement, which at first was one in fifty, then one in twenty, finally fixing it at its present point.[2] Forfeiture in case fraud was discovered was, as in the former act, again the penalty; but the Secretary of the Treasury, on the production of satisfactory evidence of innocence, might remit it. It was also

[1] From this time on until the passage of the late act, this provision that the collector " should decide between them" has been retained, though the form of the board of reappraisements was changed from time to time. It has been the subject of various interpretations which would create widely different results—the instructions of the Department for 1874 [Art. 427], being that the appraisers should make separate reports, one or the other of which the collector should adopt; but a fairer and more just rule was laid down in the General Treasury Regulations of 1884, Art. 470, which declared that the collector was not bound to adopt one or the other of the values fixed in the reports, but might determine the values as he thought just upon the testimony submitted.

[2] Subsequently (Act of July 28, 1866) he might designate a less number in certain cases where he deemed it sufficient to amply protect the revenue.

stipulated that in case a package was found to contain a less amount than that at which it was invoiced, an allowance for the same should be made in estimating the duties. Indecent prints and paintings entered might be proceeded against, seized and destroyed (§ 28).

In this act there first appears the much abused, much controverted and much litigated "similitude section." Its substance was that there should be levied on each non-enumerated article which bears a similitude, either in material, quality, texture or use, to any enumerated article, the same rate of duty levied on that article; if it resembles two or more, the highest rate applicable: and on "all articles manufactured from two or more materials, the duty should be assessed at the highest rates at which any of its component parts may be chargeable."

This section has given rise to great perplexities, and has been productive of manifold rulings by officials and courts. It is natural, and indeed indispensable, that the local customs officers should give the government the benefit of the doubt in all cases of doubtful classification,[1] not only because the collector is responsible for levying and collecting the full rate of duty, but in order to protect the revenue. For if less than the full rate is collected the security is apt to pass out of the hands of the collector before the error is corrected by the Department. Of course the effect of this is to hasten the settlement of mooted questions. But its further effect is to multiply suits upon the same question.

---

[1] In the case of Adams *vs.* Bancroft, 3 Sumner, 387, Mr. Justice Story announced that laws imposing duties are never construed beyond the natural import of the language, and duties are never imposed upon doubtful interpretation. The same principle was laid down by Mr. Justice Nelson in Powers *vs.* Booney, 3 Blatchford, 203, in which he said "that in cases of serious ambiguity in the language of the act or doubtful classification of articles, the construction is to be in favor of the importer;" and this has been adopted as the rule to govern their decisions by several Secretaries of the Treasury. In the trial of suits to overthrow the decision of the Department, the Supreme Court holds the presumption to be that the decision was correct, and the burden of disproving it is thrown upon the importer.

4

The great change that was made at this time (June 30, 1842), according to the Act of 1833, was the abolition of credits and the substitution of cash payments therefor. Its effect was immediately felt in the value of imports, but more especially in the great diminution of the amount of dutiable goods exported. In the three years following 1842, the amount thus exported was valued at only $12,590,811, being far less than in any prior three years (except during the war) since 1793, and less than in many single years immediately preceding. This marked falling off, and the intense opposition aroused among the importers to the cash payment system, again brought into prominence the idea of establishing a warehouse system, which had been more or less advocated ever since the favorable report of the Ways and Means committee in 1834. Up to this time storage had been allowed in the case of some classes of goods, but there had been no warehouse system by which payment of duties might be postponed until the goods were needed for consumption.

The Act of 1789 permitted the deposit of goods of double the value of the duties due to be made as security for their payment; in default of final payment the goods were to be sold. Of course this was intended in no sense as government storage, its object being merely to secure the revenue. The Act of 1799 permitted the importer of teas from China or Europe to deposit the imported tea for two years, at his own charge and risk, in a storehouse to be agreed upon by the importer and the inspector, the importer meantime to furnish his bond in double the amount of the duties on the tea imported. Though this was felt to be an unreasonable discrimination and elicited much criticism, it was not finally repealed until the Act of July 14, 1832. Previous to this—April 20, 1818,—a similar privilege was extended to importers of wines and distilled spirits, the term allowed for payment being shortened to one year.

This same act—July 14, 1832—allowed importers of wool or manufacturers of wool or of products of which wool was a component part, to pay the duties in cash, or at their option to place the goods in the public stores, under bond, at their own risk and subject to the payment of the customary storage charges and to the payment of interest at the rate of six per cent. per annum, while stored, the duties to be paid one half in three months and one-half in six months. If any instalment were not paid when due, so much of the goods as was necessary might be sold to meet it. The act of August 30, 1842, as has been pointed out, required that all duties be paid in cash, and in case of neglect so to do on the completion of the entry the collector might place such goods in the public stores, at the owner's charge and risk; and at the end of sixty days (ninety days if from beyond the Cape of Good Hope) [1] such quantity of the goods as should be deemed sufficient to meet the charges were to be appraised and sold by the collector at public auction.

This was the state of things when Robert J. Walker, in his first annual report as Secretary of the Treasury, strongly urged upon Congress the advisability of establishing a warehouse system; and on August 6, 1846, the act for that purpose was approved. It was based in some measure upon the English statute of 1833,[2] but left the details largely for the regulation of the Secretary of the Treasury. It permitted warehousing, at the charge and risk of the owner, of all goods (except those of a perishable character) for the period of one year,[3] the duties thereon[4] to be secured by the bond of the owner with surety in double their amount; the goods or a part of them to be at

---

[1] The period was lengthened by the act of July 30, 1846, to one year for all goods.

[2] 3 and 4 William IV. One of a series of English acts said to have been founded upon the system of Holland. See Dowell's History of Taxation in England. Index Vol. II, *Sub verbo* Warehouse.

[3] Increased to two years in case of exportation March 3, 1849, and to three years by act of 1854 ; again reduced during the war, but successively raised since, and by the act of 1890 again fixed at three years.

[4] To be estimated on entry for warehousing.

all times subject to withdrawal upon payment of the duties and other charges upon them.

Walker was an enthusiastic admirer of the English system, and by his instructions and rules regulated all matters left to his discretion in strict conformity to the English law.[1] He went very far in this and, through a somewhat strained construction of the clause giving him wide discretionary powers, introduced the system of *private* bonded warehouses, which was subsequently confirmed by the act of March 28, 1854, and has ever since remained in force.[2] Under it, as extended by this later act, goods might be deposited either in the public stores, owned or leased by the United States, in the private warehouse of the importer, used exclusively for this purpose, or in a private warehouse used exclusively as a general warehouse for the storage of warehoused goods—the place of deposit being mentioned on the entry. Such private warehouses were to be previously approved by the Secretary of the Treasury[3] and placed in charge of a government officer. All labor on the stored goods must be performed under the supervision of the officer and at the expense of the owner. The owner was further required to enter into a bond in such a sum and with such sureties as should be approved by the Secretary of the Treasury, to hold the United States and its officers harmless from any risk, loss or expense connected with the

[1] Report of February 22, 1849.

[2] The act of July 14, 1832, which was not to go into immediate effect, in order to give merchants importing goods between the time of its passage and the date set for its enforcement the advantage of the lower duties, allowed the deposit, under bond, of the goods imported up to that date in the public stores. An act supplemental to this, passed March 2, 1833, authorized the collector, as a temporary provision where the quantity of the merchandise exceeded ten packages, to allow it to remain in the warehouse of the owner if he considered the same a safe place of deposit; an officer of the customs to be placed in charge and to "keep them under the keys of the custom house." This is the first mention of private warehousing in our statutes.

[3] Held to be a privilege and not a right. The Secretary may refuse if he choose to declare a warehouse a bonded warehouse. 3 Blatchford, 113.

deposit of goods therein. Goods, by act of 1854, might remain in the warehouse three years, and at any time within
that period might be withdrawn, without payment of duties,
for exportation if entered for exportation, or on payment of
duties for consumption if entered for consumption. No abatement or allowance was made for damage, loss or leakage,
except in case of fire or other casualty and upon satisfactory
proof thereof to the Secretary of Treasury.[1]

Goods might also be withdrawn for rewarehousing else-
where, in which case a bond was required stipulating the time
and place of delivery, the transportation to be over a route approved by the Secretary of the Treasury; failure to transport
and deliver within the time specified was to subject the goods
to an additional duty of one hundred per cent.,[2] and the vessel
or vehicle transporting the same to seizure and forfeiture.

In this same year, July 30, 1846, a law was passed reducing
the old penalty of fifty per cent. in case an appraisal added ten
per cent. or upwards to the invoice value, to its present ratio
of twenty per cent. The importer was also allowed to add
such sum to the invoice on entry as he might deem sufficient
to raise the goods to their actual market value. As originally
drafted the ninth section of this act provided for a substantial
adoption of the European plan for the prevention of undervaluation.[3]   It gave the collector power, upon suspicion of fraud

---

[1] Heretofore the only redress in such cases was by special act of Congress, but
applications became very numerous, and Congress is a clumsy and unreliable re-
liever of private grievances; it goes too far when it does act, but more frequently
does not act at all.   There had constantly been appeals to Congress for remission
of fines and penalties and even duties, and each new tariff brought a fresh batch of
grievances because of inequalities or injustice arising out of the change of the old
law or incident to putting the new one into operation, especially the act of May
29, 1830.   Indeed, importers seemed to have fallen into the habit of running to
Congress continually for relief.

[2] Explained by § 20 of the act of July 14, 1862, to mean double the duties to
which the goods would have been liable on the original entry.   Statutes at Large,
Vol. IX., p. 43.

[3] French Law, 4 floréal, an IV., Law July 2, 1836; German Law of 1869,

and with the sanction of the Secretary of the Treasury, to seize the suspected goods and sell them within twenty days at auction in the manner prescribed by law for the sale of unclaimed goods, the receipts to go into the treasury, and the importer to be given a sum equal to one hundred and five per cent. of the invoice entry. This provision was stricken out on motion of Webster.

The appropriateness of such a remedy to a system of *ad valorem* duties cannot be judged from its use among the nations of Europe, whose tariff rates are in general specific. Even under a system of specific duties it is apt to do injustice to the importer, and to be of little advantage to the government. Its non-adoption with us is hardly to be deplored.

6. *The Administrative Remedy by Appeal to the Secretary of the Treasury.*

Up to this time collectors were allowed to retain certain amounts to meet suits brought against them in their official capacity. The salaries of officers were supposed to be paid out of the moneys received from fees. But for some time, where the fees were inadequate, they had been paid directly out of the revenue. This practice was abolished in 1843.

On March 3, 1839, Congress passed an act requiring that "the gross amount of all duties received from customs and from all miscellaneous sources for the use of the United States shall be paid by the officer or agent receiving the same into the treasury of the United States at as early a day as practicable, without any abatement or deduction on account of salaries, fees, costs, charges, expenses or claims of any description whatever." The Secretary of the Treasury was to submit to Congress his estimate of necessary expenses of collecting the revenue, which were to be met out of the appropriation made therefor. These expenses were limited to $1,560,000 per

Bundesgesetzblatt 1869, p. 317, § 93; *Cf.* Political Science Quarterly, Vol. I., p. 40: The Collection of Duties in the United States, by Professor Goodnow.

annum, together with such sums as were paid under the law into the treasury for drayage, labor and storage.[1]

This law further provided that if an importer should be dissatisfied with the decision of the collector as to the amount of duties, and should prove to the Secretary of the Treasury that more money had been paid to the collector than was required by law, the Secretary should draw his warrant in favor of the importer. This is the first instance of an adminstrative appeal from the decision of the collector [as to rate and amount] to the Secretary of the Treasury. After this law was passed, when a suit was brought against the collector in the old way, the court held that no suit would lie.[2]

Such a remedy appeared insufficient to Congress, which in 1845[3] repealed the law of 1839 in so far as it gave an administrative remedy by appeal to the Secretary, expressly permitted suit to be brought against the collector, and provided that the government should pay all such judgments obtained against collectors. By the act of March 3, 1857, Congress re-established the administrative remedy originally provided in 1839, in addition to the judicial remedy provided by the act of 1845. By this act it was provided that, in case the importer was dissatisfied with the decision of a collector as to the liability of goods to pay duty or their exemption therefrom, he might, on giving notice in writing of his objections to the collector within ten days after the entry, setting forth distinctly and specifically the grounds, appeal within thirty days from the date of the decision to the Secretary of the Treasury, whose decision should be final, unless suit for the duties was brought against the collector within thirty days thereafter.[4]

---

[1] In 1850 $1,000,000 was appropriated for general expenses, besides $225,000 for specific purposes. At present the regular annual appropriation for many years has been fixed at $5,500,000, with usually a large deficiency allowance.

[2] Cary v. Curtis, 3 How., 236.

[3] 5 Statutes at Large, 727.

[4] The act of June 30, 1864, extended the period for appeal to the courts to 90 days. The wording of this statute was more comprehensive, including as matters of appeal, rates and amounts of duties, fees, charges and exactions of whatever character.

In 1851[1] the law of appraisement which since its original establishment in 1823 had been modified, among other years, in 1828, 1830, 1832 and 1842, was again taken up and the President was authorized to appoint four " appraisers of mer- chandise" [general appraisers], to be allowed a salary of two thousand five hundred dollars yearly, together with actual traveling expenses, who should visit such ports as the Secretary of the Treasury might direct, and give such aid as he should think necessary. In case of appeal from the regular appraisers, the collector should select one discreet and experienced merchant to be associated with one of these appraisers, who, together, should appraise the goods, in the manner prescribed by the law of August 13, 1842. A professional element was thus introduced into the board of reappraisement, removing it still further from any influence of the importer. The merchant appraiser was to be appointed by the collector, thus retaining the principle adopted in 1842,[2] when the power of reappraisement was for the first time placed in a body in the selection of which the importer had no voice.

[1] March 3, 2d Session, 31st Congress, Chapter 39.

[2] See *supra*, p. 48.

CHAPTER IV.

TARIFF ADMINISTRATION FROM THE CIVIL WAR TO 1890.

1. Attack on the Warehouse System.

THE enormous increase in the tariff rendered necessary by the war, the high *ad valorem* rates and taxation of almost all imports, held out great allurements and high rewards for frauds upon the revenue. Stringent measures for the prevention and detection of these frauds were recognized as needful, and were enacted. Between March 1, 1861, and March 4, 1873, there were passed fourteen principal statutes relating to classification and rates, besides twenty other acts or resolutions modifying or affecting tariff acts.

The law of March 2, 1861,[1] provided that the value on which duties should be estimated should be that on the "day of actual shipment," as shown by the bill of lading, certified to by a United States consul or commercial agent.

At this time a severe attack was made on the warehouse system, as merely another method of giving credit on imports. But it was ably defended by Mr. Hunter, chairman of the Finance Committee, who declared that it was not a credit extended by the government, but was merely giving our merchants the advantage of storing on this side instead of on the other, and making our cities (instead of foreign ports)[2] the great storehouses of the country's goods. Indeed it is hard to combat the justice of an arrangement which at no risk or expense

---

[1] 36th Congress, Session II., Chapter 68.

[2] The great reason for adopting this system at the time of its establishment was to facilitate the re-exportation of dutiable goods, but neither at the time nor subsequently has the storage of goods to be re-exported been its chief function.

to the government, delays the payment of duties until the goods pass into actual use. However, the system had then, and has still more so now, become so firmly established as to safely be regarded a permanent feature of our customs machinery. Nevertheless this bill as originally passed by the House of Representatives required that duties be paid within one month from the time of entry, and that all goods in warehouses pay cash within thirty days from the passage of the bill.[1] This harsh provision was modified in committee; and as subsequently passed allowed goods to be warehoused for three months, and postponed the operations of that clause for four months. At the same time there was a strong contest over the relative merits of *ad valorem* and specific duties,[2] as a result of which there was in many cases a return to specific rates where the extreme development of the *ad valorem* principle in 1846 had applied that form of assessing duties.

The act of July 14, 1862,[3] which slightly modified the requirement of consular verification, extending it to all goods, whether subject to *ad valorem* duty or not, imposed upon the consuls the duty of reporting any suspicious or fraudulent acts of foreign consignors. It also changed the provisions for storage, lengthening the time for payment of duties on warehoused goods to one year and allowing the goods to remain for three years; if left longer they were to be deemed abandoned. It was further provided that on all goods exported within those three years ninety-nine per cent. of the duties already paid should be returned.[4]

[1] There were probably from fifty to sixty million dollars worth of goods in warehouses at that time, and from ten to twelve million dollars of duties due thereon —the passage of this provision would have precipitated a financial crisis among importers.

[2] Any one in search of remarkable displays of Congressional mastery of administrative problems should read the vigorous arguments of this date, to prove that an *ad valorem* tax is easier and cheaper to collect and less capable of being avoided than a specific tax.

[3] 37th Congress, Session II., Chapter 163.

[4] Act of August 5, 1861, fixed the drawback at ninety per cent. of the duties paid. 37th Congress, Session I., Chapter. 45.

2. *Triplicate Invoices.*

On March 3, 1863,[1] the President approved the most stringent measure ever applied in our service to the purpose declared by its title, viz, " to prevent and punish frauds upon the
revenue," *etc.* It provided that after the succeeding July all
invoices of goods should be made in triplicate and should have
inclosed thereon a declaration[2] signed by the owner, purchaser,
manufacturer or agent, setting forth the price or cost and time
and place of purchase or manufacture, about as prescribed by
the previous laws. These invoices should be produced to the
consular officer nearest the place of shipment, and the owner,
importer or agent, *etc.*, should then declare to the said consul,
vice-consul or commercial agent, the port at which it was intended to make entry of the goods. Thereupon the consular
officer was to endorse upon each of the triplicates a certificate
stating that the invoice on that date had been produced to him,
the name of the person producing it, and the port in the
United States where entry was intended to be made.[3] This
officer was to give one of the triplicates to the person producing them, to be used in making entry; he was to file and
preserve one in his office; and speedily transmit the third to
the collector of the port designated as the intended port of
entry.[4] Goods should not be admitted to entry unless the invoice conformed to these requirements.

[1] 37th Congress, Session II., Chapter 76.

[2] Heretofore, by the law of 1823, this must be sworn to, but by this the simple
declaration was sufficient. But the law of March 3, 1865, allowed the consular
officers to require " satisfactory evidence either by oath * * or otherwise that
such invoices were correct and true," and they were instructed by the Secretary
of State to do this, " whenever they deemed it expedient," by examining under
oath any person whose statements would be of value " upon any matters " ger-
mane to the subject of inquiry.

[3] This is the consular authentication as distinct from the owner's verification.

[4] If goods arrived before the receipt by the collector of his triplicate, they
might be entered, on bond of double the apparent amount of duties being given,
to await the arrival of the triplicate or a certified copy thereof.

For entry under a false invoice or certificate the goods or their value should be forfeited, the penalty to be divided as other forfeitures were. The Solicitor of the Treasury[1] was required to look after all frauds and attempted frauds upon the revenue. Frauds were punishable by imprisonment for a term not to exceed two years, and by a fine of not more than five thousand dollars. The punishment also included removal from office in case a customs officer was implicated. It was made the duty of the district attorney, by § 13, to defend all suits brought against collectors or other officers of the revenue for their official acts.

Up to this date the chief officer of any port or his appointee on getting a warrant therefor from a justice of the peace, might, enter any private premises not unreasonably remote from the coast, search for and seize any goods on which all the duties had not been paid, and examine and remove for inspection any books or papers containing information with regard to such goods.[2] The act of 1863 (§ 7) placed this power in the hands of the United States District Judge, who was authorized to issue such a warrant to the collector only upon proof by affidavit to his satisfaction that fraud had been actually committed or attempted. The invoices, books or papers so seized were to be retained by the officer seizing them, subject to the control and direction of the Solicitor of the Treasury.

This dangerous power was subsequently further restricted on July 18, 1866, and March 2, 1867.[3] According to these laws the warrant was directed to the United States District Marshal instead of to the collector, and the papers were to be subject to the disposition of the court instead of the Solicitor of the Treasury.

---

[1] This office was established by the law of May 29, 1830.

[2] § 68 of the law of 1799.

[3] 39th Congress Session II., Chapter 188. This act provided for the distribution of fines and penalties, giving carriers a lien for freight which could be enforced before the release of the debtor's goods from the warehouse, when previous notice had been given to the collector.

3. Dutiable Value.

The increase in duties in 1864[1] was accompanied by slight changes in the collection laws. The method of determining the dutiable value was again defined, this time as[2] "the actual value of such goods on shipboard at the last place of shipment to the United States," and was to be ascertained by adding to " the value of such goods, at the place of growth or manufacture, the cost of transportation, shipment, trans-shipment, with all expenses included, the value of the sack, box, or covering of any kind, commissions at the usual rate, in no case less than two and a half per cent., brokerage and export duties, together with all costs and charges." This finally settled a moot point in the law of 1851 (March 3), and put an end to the contention on which, up to that time, over fourteen hundred suits had been brought against the collector at New York, viz., that under the former law no account should be taken of commissions and certain charges.[3]

The last section of this act allowed baggage or personal effects arriving in the United States in transit for a foreign country to be deposited with the collector, to be retained and delivered by him to the parties having it in charge on their

[1] June 30, 1864, 38th Congress Session I., Chapter 171.

[2] Over this there was a difference of opinion and on its substantial reënactment in 1866 there was a sharp contest; in the Senate Mr. Sherman attacked it as bearing too heavily on bulky goods, and introducing so many elements into the estimated cost as to render it uncertain, thus giving rise to frauds and perhaps inequality.

Mr. Edmunds on the other hand upheld it, saying that all tariffs were based on home value, and that these were its necessary elements. On the vote it was stricken out; but as the House did not agree, it was retained in the above form.

[3] Under the law of 1851 the Secretary of the Treasury had made a ruling that certain charges, including commissions at two and a half per cent., should be items in estimating dutiable value. This caused a vast amount of litigation, and many of these cases, commonly called the "charges and commissions cases," remained pending down through the seventies. The government was compelled to pay out several millions in judgments—the items of interest and costs forming a large proportion of the total amount.

departure for their foreign destination, under such rules as the Secretary of the Treasury might prescribe.

4. *Appraisement at New York.*

On July 27, 1866, the matter of appraisement at the port of New York,[1] was again taken up, and as fixed by this law has remained substantially the system of appraisement at that port to this day.[2]

In lieu of the appraisers formerly stationed there, the president was authorized to appoint one appraiser who had had experience as such, and with the same qualifications heretofore required of the several appraisers.[3] This officer was to have supervision of examinations, inspection and appraisements. Under him were to be not exceeding ten assistant appraisers, appointed by the Secretary of the Treasury, and with qualifications similar to those required of the appraiser. Their report, approved by the appraiser, was to be regarded as the legal appraisement.[4]

In lieu of the clerks at this time employed in the examination of goods, the Secretary of the Treasury was to appoint, on nomination of the appraiser, such number of examiners as he might determine to be necessary. These examiners were to be " practically and thoroughly acquainted with the character, quality and value " of the articles in the examination of which they were employed. Their compensation was not to exceed two thousand five hundred dollars yearly.[5]

The Secretary was also to appoint, on nomination of the appraiser, the clerks, verifiers, samplers, openers, packers and

---

[1] 39th Congress, Session I., Chapter 284.

[2] Other ports are governed in this matter by various statutes, but the main facts of the system excepting the names of officers are practically the same.

[3] See *supra*, pp. 34 and 42.

[4] Their duties were apportioned among them, each having a particular department, as special examiner of drugs, appraiser of damaged goods, *etc.*

[5] The appraiser's salary was fixed at $4,000, and that of the assistant appraisers at $3,000 each.

messengers employed in the appraiser's office, and to fix their number and compensation. The old laws as to the manner of valuation and appraisement were to apply as before.

5. *Transportation in Bond.*

The act of July 28, of this same year,[1] authorized the Secretary of the Treasury to appoint certain ports at which goods destined for Canada or Mexico might be entered and transported in bond to their destination through the territory of the United States, under such regulations as might be prescribed. Goods subject to duty might also be transported across the territories of those countries, with the consent of the proper authorities, in transit from one place in the United States to another, over such routes and under such regulations as the Secretary should prescribe.

The law of July 14, 1870,[2] farther perfected this system of bonded transportation. According to its provisions goods destined for certain interior points—about one to each state— when entered at specified ports, and after they had been sufficiently examined [without removal to warehouse or appraiser's office] in order to roughly verify the invoice, might be immediately shipped to their destination, provided a bond be given, with at least two sureties, for double the invoice value of the merchandise with the duties added. The formal entry, appraisement and payment of duties could then take place at the place of final distribution.[3] Such merchandise should be delivered only to common carriers designated by the Secretary of the Treasury, who were to give such bonds and in such amounts as the Secretary might require, and who were to be responsible for the safe delivery of the goods to the collector at the port of destination. The goods while in transit were not to be unladen or trans-shipped, but should be conveyed in cars,

[1] 39th Congress, Session I., Chapter 298.

[2] 41stCongress, Session II., Chapter 225.

[3] Amended, but very slightly changed, by Act of July 2, 1884, 48th Congress, Session I, Chapter 142.

vessels or vehicles securely fastened with locks or seals under the exclusive control of the officers of the customs.[1] For greater safety inspectors might be placed at proper points along the routes, or upon the trains or cars, at the expense of the respective companies.[2]

6 *Special Agents and General Orders.*

On May 11, 1870,[3] Congress passed the first law distinctly authorizing the appointment of special agents of the Treasury to be employed in the customs service. The act limited the number to be appointed to fifty-two, and divided them into three classes, with salaries running from eight dollars down to five dollars a day.[4] Already at this time there were some fifty-one such agents receiving salaries—besides expenses and mileage—from five thousand dollars down. Under what authority these men were employed is not exactly clear,[5] but the custom of appointing them seems to have obtained almost from the establishment of the government.

The influence of special agents on the department and on the development of the system is hard to estimate. It is principally through them that the Secretary comes in contact with the local service. Some such officers are absolutely necessary for the efficiency of the system; and the Secretaries unite in declaring them indispensable to the proper supervision of the local officers. They certainly have had a great inflence in cen-

[1] Any person breaking the locks or seals, or in any way gaining access to the goods with the intent of unlawfully removing them, may be imprisoned for not less than six months nor more than two years.

[2] By the treaty of March 1, 1873, a like privilege of exporting goods through the United States was given to Canada.

[3] 41st Congress, Session II., Chapter 98.

[4] The maximum number allowed was subsequently [August 15, 1876] reduced to 20, and again [June 19, 1878] raised to 28, where the limit remains to-day.

[5] The only ground on which their appointment could be legally justified would be that implied from the twenty-first section of the law of 1799, that collectors, naval officers, *etc.*, should "at all times submit their books, papers and accounts to the inspection of such persons as might be appointed for that purpose."

tralizing the customs administration, and through them the actions of collectors have been subjected to a strict central administrative control.[1]

Attention had been called to these agents by the extravagant sums paid them and by their marked inefficiency. In other words, the office had got into politics. Attention was not confined to this branch of the service alone. Investigating committees were appointed, and during the next few years the management of the New York custom house for several administrations past was examined without bringing great credit upon any one connected with it. One of the great fields for extortion from importers had been the " general order business " as it was called. In order to facilitate the sailing of vessels making regular trips, the law had long allowed them to make application to the collector, who would thereupon issue a general order that after five days all goods on board should be landed and taken into the possession of the custom house officials. This period was shortened in 1854 to three days, and in 1861 to a single day. As the time allowed to remove goods became shorter, the amount left to be taken to the government " general order stores " greatly increased. The importers were compelled to pay the charges for storage and cartage from the vessel to the stores. As the treasury regulations with regard to the matter were very loose, the management of this business was left largely to the collector. He farmed out the general order business in such a manner that the importers were subjected to exorbitant charges and poor accommodations. Monopolies such as the cartage bureau were created, which though licensed by the collector were allowed to demand inordinately high pay for services which the importers were bound to accept.[2] This, perhaps, was much more a fault in the service than in the system.

[1] See report of Secretary Manning on Collection of Duties, 1885, p. 38.

[2] House Report, No. 30, 39th Congress, Session II.; Senate Report, No. 227, 42d Congress, Session II.; Senate Report, No. 380, 41st Congress, Session III.

5

By the twenty-fourth section this great source of scandal—the general order business—was put into the hands of the Secretary of the Treasury, together with the control and regulation of the bonded warehouses. The officers of the customs were forbidden to have any personal ownership of or interest in either the bonded warehouses or the general order stores. The cartage of merchandise was to be let under regulations approved by the Secretary of the Treasury to the lowest responsible bidder who might give sufficient security.

7. Searches and Seizures.

The provision of the old law which had allowed the entry into private premises on a warrant, and the seizure of private books and papers for the purpose of obtaining information on which to bring suit of frauds intended or accomplished, was totally abolished. In lieu of the similar provision in case of suits already begun, it was provided that after suits for forfeiture had been actually commenced, the attorney for the government might make a written motion describing the desired book, paper or invoice, and setting forth the allegations that he expected to prove ; and thereupon the court in which the suit or proceeding was pending might at its discretion issue a notice to the defendant or claimant to produce the desired document at a day and hour prescribed in the notice. This notice was to be duly served by a United States Marshal, and if the defendant or claimant failed to produce the document, or to explain his failure satisfactorily, the allegation stated in the motion should be taken as confessed. If the document were produced, the government attorney should be permitted to examine it and offer the same in evidence. But the document should remain in the custody of the owner or his agent, subject to the order of the court. This entirely took away the great facilities formerly offered for obtaining evidence in the preparation of a suit, and greatly limited the opportunity for procuring evidence during the prosecution of the suit. Previous to 1874, by the law of 1799, in suits brought for violation of any provision of the customs revenue laws, if a probable cause for such prosecution was shown to the court, the burden of proof in establishing the innocence of the act was upon the party defendant. But by this law, the questions whether the alleged acts were done with the actual intent to defraud the United States were to be passed upon by the court or jury as a separate finding of fact. And unless intent to defraud should be found no fine, penalty or forfeiture was to be imposed. [1] This law was also interpreted [2] to cover the whole ground of frauds on the revenue, and to do away with the action formerly allowed for the value of goods tainted with fraud, but which had been withdrawn from the custody of the government. [3]

Any person accused of a violation of the customs revenue laws might make a petition to the judge of the district where the violation occurred, setting forth the facts of the case and praying relief. The judge might thereupon, if the case in his judgment required it, fix a time and place at which the collector and district attorney should be notified to attend and show cause why the petition should not be granted. This summary investigation should be held before the judge or a United States Commissioner and the petition with a certified copy of the evidence should be transmitted to the Secretary of the Treasury, who might mitigate or remit the fines and direct the discontinuance of the prosecution as he deemed it just. Suits for the recovery of a fine or penalty must be brought within three years, and whenever duties should have been liquidated and paid, such settlement in the absence of fraud or

[1] Section 4 of the act of May 28, 1830, required that in order to obtain a verdict for the government, it must be found that the invoices were made with intent to defraud the government. Section 1 of the act of March 3, 1863, required that in order to obtain such a verdict it must be found that the false invoice or other paper was made knowingly. But the Supreme Court still held (3 Wallace 114), that it was thrown on the claimant of the goods seized to dispel the suspicion, and to explain the circumstances which indicated that there had been knowing under-valuation.

[2] 19 Federal Reporter, p. 893.

[3] This section was repealed by act of 1890.

protest by the importer should be conclusive after the expiration of one year.   In case of fraud in the invoices, only the package containing the merchandise to which the fraud related should be forfeited.

8. *Compensation of Customs Officers.*

This act, also, partially inaugurated a much needed reform in the manner of compensating officers.   At the time of the establishment of the system it was thought that the customs service would be practically self-supporting.   With this end in view, the act of 1779 laid down a set of fees to be exacted from all who had dealings with the customs service, for the benefit of the customs officers.   In addition thereto the officers received only nominal salaries.

These fees, gathered from various sources and for various services, differed slightly in different districts, ranging in amount from ten cents to several dollars, the major portion being in sums of fifty cents and less.   The plan was never successful, and the system was at no time self-sustaining.   The multitude of small fees, though inadequate in most cases to compensate the officer, yet in busy ports amounted in the aggregate to sums which, in some instances, rewarded the officers beyond all desert.   To remedy this, the twenty-third section of this act provided that in lieu of all "salaries, moieties, and perquisites of whatever nature," the collectors, naval officers and surveyors of the principal ports were to receive the fixed salaries named therein.[1]   Why the system of salaries was not extended to all ports at this time does not appear.   That it should have been so extended has been recognized by all officials familiar with the workings of the law.   Action to this effect has been repeatedly recommended by the different Secretaries of the Treasury in their reports to Congress.

[1] Collector of New York, $12,000; collectors of Boston and Philadelphia, $8,000; collectors of San Francisco, Baltimore and New Orleans, $7,000; collector of Portland, Me., $6,000: the naval officer and surveyor at New York, each $8,000; naval officer at Boston, San Francisco, and Philadelphia, $5,000.

These fees were for the most part made up of small and vexatious exactions, difficult to collect, and involving a large amount of unprofitable clerical work in the accounts. They were also uncertain. For instance, the allowance for storage, for which no equivalent service was rendered, might be retained by the collector to the amount of two thousand dollars, if the sum amounted to so much. Under the complicated system of computation adopted, this system opened wide the way for fraud, at least in the smaller districts. Many collectors on the northern, northeastern and northwestern frontiers received more from the sale of blanks to the railway companies[1] than from their salaries. In some instances the income from this source has exceeded the official salary by ten or fifteen thousand dollars. Furthermore, the income to the government from this source is comparatively meagre, being less than a quarter of a million dollars in recent years.

9. Repeal of the Moieties Clause.

About this time the numerous prosecutions of importers for fraud and the immense sums recovered by revenue officers and informers[2] in these suits, as well as the vigorous and unscrupulous enforcement of the harsh provisions of the law by officers interested in the resulting penalties, raised a general and just clamor for a change in the law.[3] The scandals of these proceedings were indeed very great, the hardships upon some innocent importers very severe, while the vexation, annoyance and apprehension of all were deplorable.

The Secretary of Treasury wrote a letter to Congress advocating the abolition of moieties and many fines;[4] the Con-

[1] Permitted by § 2648 of the Revised Statutes.

[2] Collectors at New York received from this source: May 1866 to March 1869, $102,710; April 1869 to July 1870, $41,304; July 1870 to Nov. 1871, $55,997; Dec. 1871 to Nov. 1873, $56,120.

[3] House Report 111, 38th Congress, Session I. History of Proceedings in the case of Phelps, Dodge & Co. Miscellaneous Document No. 264, 43d Congress, Session I. House Report No. 30, 39th Congress, Session II.

[4] Executive Document No. 283, 41st Congress, Session II.

gressional Committees recommended the same action. As a result the law of June 22, 1874, was passed. By it all provisions by which moieties had been allowed were repealed, and the proceeds of all fines, penalties and forfeitures were ordered to be paid into the United States Treasury. In cases of the detection of smuggling, and in such cases only, the informer or officer might be allowed such compensation as the Secretary of the Treasury should award—not to exceed five thousand dollars.

Although the law contained numerous changes, its main object and principal result were the abolition of "moieties," with the view to deter officers from bringing and pressing suits in the hope of obtaining a share in the severe and often disproportionate penalties exacted. The law has more than fulfilled its purpose. It is an open question whether Congress did not go too far in the matter, and by removing all strong personal interest leading persons to undertake the risk and labor of bringing prosecutions, open wide the door to frauds and consequent injustice to the honest importer for whose protection this very law was framed. The falling off in the amount received from fines, penalties and forfeitures was immediate and marked.[1] In the ten years preceding 1874, there had been brought in the Southern District of New York 957 suits or proceedings, on which $3,696,232.53 were paid into the registry of the court. In the ten years following 1874, 254 suits were begun, and thereon only $393,774.72 were paid into the registry of the court. Yet during the latter period imports vastly increased; and there is no reason,— indeed the tendency of the law would in effect have been the very opposite,—to believe that under-valuation was any less prevalent. B. H. Bristow, Secretary of the Treasury, in his annual report for the year 1874, deplored the action of Con-

[1] Proceeds from this source paid into the Treasury from 1870–1877: Year ending June 20, 1871, $952,579.86; 1872, $674,232.77; 1873, $1,169,515.38; 1874, (law went into effect June 22), $651,271.76; 1875, $228,870.23; 1876, $183,797.86; 1877, $146,413.21.

gress in this matter. Ever since that time there has been a continual demand from the Secretaries of the Treasury for more adequate legislation for the prevention of frauds upon the revenue.

10. Repeal of Discrimination against Goods from the Far East.

The Acts of May 4, 1882, and December 23, 1882,[1] repealed the provision of the Act of December 31st, 1862, which levied a discriminating duty of ten per cent. additional upon all goods, wares and merchandise, of the growth or product of the countries east of the Cape of Good Hope, when imported from places west of that Cape. The object of this law had been the fostering of direct commerce with the Orient, carried on in American bottoms. But the opening of the Suez Canal had changed the course of Eastern commerce, which now naturally flowed through this gateway into the European markets. As a consequence, it became much cheaper to bring these goods *viâ* the European ports, and it was often very difficult to determine whether goods purchased in Europe were originally from the East or not. The resulting confusion and uncertainty, with no adequate corresponding benefit, rendered the repeal of the act advisable. We see in this a curious instance of how seemingly independent occurrences may affect our administrative problems.

11. Dutiable Value and Similitude Section under the Act of 1883.

The tariff Act of March 3, 1883[2] had appended to it several sections governing administrative matters. It contained new and lengthy forms of oaths: first, of the consignee, importer, or agent, to be taken on entry; second, of the owner when the goods had been purchased; and third, of the manufacturer when they had not been purchased. But the forms

---

[1] 47th Congress, Session I., Chapter 120; 47th Congress, Session II., Chapter 6.
[2] 47th Congress, Session II, Chapter 121.

added little that had not been contained in, or implied by, the oaths formerly required.

The previous law, which provided that the usual and necessary " sacks, crates, boxes or coverings " be estimated as part of the value of imported goods, was repealed; and such charges were not thereafter to be included, in determining the amount of duties for which goods were liable.   As the " dutiable value " of goods was declared by the same act to be their " actual market value," or their actual wholesale price in the condition of finish and preparation for sale in which they were finally offered by the foreign merchant to his customers, and as many kinds of goods were never offered for sale and had no market value except as prepared for shipment with their proper coverings, the question at once arose : At what valuation should these goods be entered for duty?   A variance of opinions and practice speedily sprang up.   The Treasury Department, under Mr. Folger, ruled that coverings, *etc.*, should be included as forming part of the value of the goods.   This decision was subsequently upheld by the court.[1]   The decisions and instructions of the Department resulted, however, in a large number of protests and the bringing of many suits.

The " similitude" section of the existing law, originally enacted in 1842, was reënacted in a more elaborate form, and with the added proviso that " non-enumerated articles similar in material and quality and texture and the use to which they may be applied, to articles on the free list, and in the manufacture of which no dutiable materials shall be used, shall be free."   The section, even under a generous interpretation by the Secretary, gave rise to considerable additional litigation. Collectors were still perplexed over the term " market value," in spite of all the defining legislation.   Importers who received special goods under consignment even claimed that those goods had no market value.   To meet this contention section nine of this act provided that if it should appear that the true and actual

---

[1] 24 Federal Reporter, 852.

wholesale price could not be ascertained to the satisfaction of the appraiser, it should be lawful to appraise the merchandise by ascertaining the cost or value of the materials composing it at the time and place of manufacture, together with the cost of manufacturing, preparing and putting up for shipment. This ought to have definitely settled the old "no market value" claim; but it was too specious to be given up thus easily, and we find it urged again and again by contesting consignees of dutiable goods.[1]

12. Classification of Sugars under the Act of 1883.

Schedule E of the act, relating to sugars, prescribed that the different grades should pay duties according to the Dutch standard of color, to be determined by their "polariscopic test." This was the mere legislative adoption of the form of test already prescribed by the Secretary of the Treasury. On account of the general practice of artificially coloring sugar in order to lower its apparent "Dutch color standard" on which by law it was to pay duty, the Secretary had found it necessary to rule that all sugars be classified by their " natural color," as he called it, that is, by their saccharine strength as determined by the polariscope. The fraud had been very widespread and profitable, and this action of the Secretary naturally gave rise to a great many suits against the government. The government had also brought suit against the importers for fraud. But on account of the great difficulty of proving guilty knowledge as required under the law of 1874, no penalties could be enforced, although fraud was notorious. Sugar was always a very troublesome article to list properly. It seems from the first to have furnished a fruitful field for gigantic frauds upon the revenue. One of the earlier methods which had proved very successful had been the importation of cane juice boiled nearly to

---

[1] The effect of this clause, if it had any, was found to be an increase in the efforts of manufacturers to conceal the price at which they held their goods abroad and to throw upon the appraisers, few of whom had the requisite skill or experience, the burden of ascertaining the cost of manufacture.

the point of crystallization, or of any solution holding a large amount of sugar, as molasses or syrup, which bore a much lighter duty than sugar.   Even since the use of the polariscope, grave and suspicious differences have existed between the tests at different ports.

13. Passengers' Baggage.

The law of 1883 again enacted the provision of the former law, exempting from taxation " wearing apparel in actual use and other personal effects," *etc.*[1]   The interpretation of this clause has been very liberal,[2] but is necessarily so indefinite as to give rise to much contention and hard feeling.   The examination of passengers' baggage is, from its nature, one of the most troublesome functions of the inspection service.   It is the point where the government must go deepest into the private affairs of those with whom it deals; and it is consequently productive of great friction.   The wonderful increase in the trans-Atlantic passenger trade, composed in large measure of tourists carrying extensive wardrobes, has added to the difficulties of this service.   It has usually been performed on the various steamship wharves, although for a time it was carried on at the barge office in New York.   No place is prescribed by law, and in order to expedite matters and to cause as little annoyance and delay as possible to travelers, who would presumably suffer considerable inconvenience if their baggage were long detained, this scattered manner of conducting the

---

[1] See *supra*, page 30.

[2] Astor *v.* Meritt, 111 U. S. 202, defined the terms as follows : " Wearing apparel owned by the passenger and in condition to be worn at once without further manufacture; (2) brought with him as a passenger and intended for the use or wear of himself or his family who accompanied him as passengers, and not for sale or purchase, or imported for other persons or to be given away; (3) suitable for the season of year which was immediately approaching at the time of the arrival; (4) not exceeding in quantity, or quality, or value, what the passenger was in the habit of ordinarily providing for himself and his family at that time, and keeping on hand for his and their reasonable wants, in view of their means and habits of life, even though such articles had not been actually worn." By no means an easy thing for the inspector to find out !

inspection has been maintained. On the other hand, it has unquestionably rendered supervision so difficult that in spite of the efforts of the Treasury Department, the practice of bribe-taking, or the "acceptance of gifts" by the inspectors from arriving passengers is very general, and produces a very demoralizing effect.

CHAPTER V.

THE McKINLEY ADMINISTRATION BILL OF 1890.

1. General Purposes of the Late Acts.

THE next important measure affecting the customs administration was the Act of June 10, 1890. During the recent discussion of the tariff by Congress, the several bills that were introduced contained in every instance provisions, drafted either directly by the Treasury Department or with its advice and sanction, intended to meet the defects which had been repeatedly pointed out by the different Secretaries in the existing law regulating customs administration.

There were many ambiguities and conflicting provisions in the tariff schedules which had been for many years constant subjects of dispute and litigation; perhaps the most notorious of these was the discrimination between worsteds and woolens. On account of changes in manufacturing processes, these had become so nearly identical in use that the difference in duties on practically the same goods might vary nearly twenty-five per cent., according as they could be put into one class or the other. These matters are not, strictly speaking, administrative questions. But they have such a great bearing upon the ease, economy and exactness of the service, and such a deep influence on the popular temper towards it—since close distinctions breed hard feelings and litigation—that it must be regretted that they are so little considered from this standpoint.

The administrative bill of 1890 was not an attempt to secure a general revision of customs laws and regulations, but merely another patch to the existing piece-work system, consisting of the surviving provisions of hundreds of acts,[1] rulings and

---

[1] In 1889, Mr. Windom said the laws regulating the collection of duties were

regulations, the result of nearly one hundred years of legislative and administrative activity. Such a body of laws must be unwieldy, disconnected and disproportioned; and a careful and complete codification, reconciling conflicting provisions and ambiguities, would do much towards increasing the ease of executing the law, would serve to point out its defects and gaps, and would at least render it possible to ascertain definitely the exact statements of the law on any point. This would be no small service in the way of diminishing litigation, the amount of which in recent years has been little short of appalling. For a number of years previous to the passage of the last act, suits were brought in the United States circuit court for the southern district of New York on customs questions, at the rate of about fifteen hundred annually, and were disposed of at about one-third that rate; some five thousand cases had accumulated on the calendar, involving, it is estimated, over twenty-five million dollars, with no good prospect of their being disposed of in the next decade. The delay not only injures honest importers, but by throwing the defense of all suits brought under one administration upon the succeeding ones, provokes lax methods, allows the loss of evidence and in the end must result in unjust judgments against the government, in which case the government is compelled to pay heavy costs and interest for a number of years at six per cent. The unnecessary loss involved in this operation may easily be calculated; for the government is able at any time to borrow money at approximately two per cent.

As has been noticed, the earlier acts contained no restrictions as to the size, shape and markings of imported packages, except wine and spirits; gradually others crept in, as those upon tobacco and cigars. The last act went farther than any of its predecessors in so far as it required that unpolished cylinder crown and common window glass, imported

derived from 263 different Acts of Congress, passed during the preceding ninety years.

in boxes, should contain fifty square feet, and that unless all articles of foreign manufacture such as are usually or ordinarily marked, stamped, branded or labelled, and all packages containing such or other imported articles should respectively be so marked, *etc.*, " in legible English words, so as to indicate the country of their origin," they should not be admitted to entry. Provisions of this nature may be of undoubted value and assistance to custom officers, but they are sure to be resented and may amount to a severe hardship upon importers; and, if too much extended, would even constitute a restriction upon trade. Indeed, this last provision, which was to go into effect on March 1, 1891, thus giving nine months' notice, has been found to be so little understood and to work such obvious injustice upon innocent violators, that the Department has ruled that it will not be enforced where the disregard of it has been through excusable ignorance or mistake.

A provision of the old law, which had been found very difficult of interpretation and productive of many protests and suits, required non-enumerated articles manufactured from two or more materials to pay duty at the highest rate that would be chargeable if composed "wholly of the component material of chief value." This was here further explained. The term, " component material of chief value," was defined as " that component material which shall exceed in value any other single component material of the article."[1]

2. Increased Stringency of Provisions to Prevent Fraud.

Like former laws, the administrative bill proper[2] requires consular verification of invoices, to be made out before the

---

[1] It had been variously contended that this clause should mean the most expensive kind of material used, and as held in the text; further, there had been great doubt as to when that value should be estimated, whether before manufacture, or as found in the article. The latter rule was by this law declared the correct one.

[2] In treating of the acts of 1890, for convenience, no distinction has been made, except in the references, between the Administrative Act approved June 10 and the Tariff Act approved Oct. 2.

same officers and in practically the same form in triplicate,
or in quadruplicate if intended for immediate trans-shipment
to interior points.   Invoices made out according to the provisions of this act must, as before, be produced on entry;
although, as formerly, when the importer makes affidavit
showing the reasons accompanied by a statement in the form
of an invoice, he may make entry without having a duly certified invoice provided that the collector is satisfied that the
failure to produce it is due to causes beyond his control.

This *pro forma* invoice must be verified by the oath of the
importer, who may also be examined under oath by the collector as to the sources of his information in the premises,
and who may be required to produce any letter, paper or
statement of account under his control which may assist the
officers in ascertaining the value of the importation.   But the
great and much-needed change was that merchandise entered
on a *pro forma* invoice is subjected to the same conditions,
fines, forfeitures, *etc.*, as are imposed in case of entry upon
"original" or regularly certified invoices.[1]   The three forms
of declaration required on entry respectively of the agent, the
purchasing owner or the manufacturer, are much the same as
those in the law of 1883; except that " value " in each case is
defined at length as being the " actual market value or wholesale price at the time of exportation to the United States, in
the principal markets of the country from whence imported,
and including the value of all cartons, cases, crates, boxes,
sacks and coverings of any kind, and all other charges and
expenses incident to placing said goods in condition, packed
ready for shipment to the United States."

Thus the position taken in 1883, of exempting coverings, *etc.*,
which had been greatly modified in practice, was definitely
abandoned.[2]   The changes in the declarations were made so that

---

[1] Prior to this the exemption of *pro forma* invoices from these liabilities had
been, in the eyes of the customs officers, a temptation to undervaluation not
always successfully resisted.

[2] The peculiar forms of coverings sometimes used since the law of 1883, sug-

they would conform to and harmonize with the requirements in respect to entry. It is further provided by the seventh section that where the appraised value of any merchandise shall exceed its invoice value by more than ten per cent., there shall be levied on such merchandise—not on the whole invoice—two per cent. additional for each one per cent. of excess over the declared value. If the appraised value exceeds the entry value by more than forty per cent., such entry shall be deemed presumptively fraudulent and the collector may seize the goods. In any resulting legal proceedings the burden of proof shall be on the claimant to rebut the presumption of fraud by sufficient evidence. And in all suits or informations brought where property is seized pursuant to the customs collection laws, the burden of proof shall lie on the claimant of the property, provided that probable cause is shown for such prosecution, to be judged by the court. (§ 21.) This method was adopted because of the practical impossibility of securing a judgment under the law of 1874, which compelled the government to prove fraudulent intent in all cases. It was very difficult for the government to do this, since all the papers, *etc.*, concerning the transaction were in the hands of the importer, and were, by the same law, obtainable only in part and by a clumsy process.[1]

In case goods are consigned by the manufacturer to any person in the United States, such person on their entry shall present to the collector, in addition to the verified invoice, a statement signed by the manufacturer, declaring the cost of their production. (§ 8.)[2]   Where goods are consigned by a person

gested the added clause, "if there be used for covering * * * any unusual article or form designed for use otherwise than in the *bona fide* transportation * * * duty shall be levied upon such article or material at the rate to which the same would be subject if separately imported."

[1] See *supra* p. 66.

[2] § 11 declares that when the appraiser cannot to his satisfaction ascertain the market value of goods, he may estimate their *cost of production*, such cost to include "cost of materials and fabrication, all general expenses covering each and every

other than the manufacturer a like statement must be presented, signed by the consignor and declaring that the said
goods were purchased by or for him, showing the time when,
the place where, and the person from whom they were purchased, and giving in detail the price paid for the same. These
statements must be attested by a consular officer, filed and
transmitted in the same manner as are invoices.

3. Remedies against Appraisement and Classification.

Pursuant to the recommendations of several of the Secretaries of the Treasury, the number of general appraisers was
increased. This office had been created for the purpose of
correcting the inequalities in appraisement at the different
ports. The general appraiser was to exercise a general supervision over appraisement, more especially to act with a merchant as a board of reappraisement. But the duties were too
numerous and the number of officers too limited; in some instances only a single officer was assigned to over fifty different
districts and ports.

By the present act the President is authorized to appoint
nine such officers, at a salary of seven thousand dollars each,
not more than five to be from the same political party.

Three of their number shall be on duty daily as a board of
general appraisers at the port of New York, at which port
there shall be a place for samples under their care. In any
case where the collector deems the appraisement, as reported
to him by the appraiser, too low, or where the importer
within two days thereafter gives written notice of his dissatisfaction therewith, the collector shall order the goods to be
appraised by one of the general appraisers. If either party is
still dissatisfied (and in case it be the importer, only upon

outlay of whatsoever nature incident to such production, together with the expense
of preparing and putting up such merchandise ready for shipment, and an addition of eight per cent. upon the total cost, as thus ascertained." To expect a manufacturer to thus reveal his business affairs and management would be preposter-
ous, and the attempt has been found to be of but little practical utility and an
obstruction of legitimate business. See Finance Reports 1890, p. xxxiii.

6

notice as before) the collector shall transmit the invoice and all the papers appertaining thereto to the board of general appraisers.[1] These shall examine and decide the case, and the decision of a majority of them is to be final and conclusive as to *dutiable value*.

As before, the decision of the collector as to *rate* and *amount* of duty is final, unless notice of dissatisfaction be given within ten days. When such notice is received, the collector must transmit all the papers in the matter to the board of general appraisers, who shall examine and decide the case thus submitted. The decision of the board is final and conclusive, unless within thirty days the collector or the importer file in the office of the clerk of the Circuit Court of the United States for the district a concise statement of the errors of law and fact complained of, and serve a copy of the same upon the other party. Thereupon the court must order the board of appraisers to make a return of the record and evidence taken by them, together with a certified statement of the facts involved and their decision thereon. The court may within twenty days after this return, and upon application of the party, refer it to one of the general appraisers, who is to take and return such further evidence as may be offered within sixty days thereafter by the Secretary of the Treasury, the collector or the importer. Such further evidence, together with the returns, shall constitute the record upon which "the said court shall give priority to[2] and proceed to hear and determine" the questions involved. This decision is final, unless the court or judge making it, deeming the question of sufficient importance, shall within thirty days thereafter allow an appeal to be taken to the Supreme Court of the United States.

[1] Either the regular board at New York or a board of three which shall be designated by the Secretary of the Treasury for such duty, at that port or any other port.

[2] It had been the custom of the courts to give only a few days in each term to the consideration of these cases, which accounts in large measure for the increasing number of cases standing over in the southern district of New York.

The general appraisers may administer oaths, may cite any person to appear before them, may require the production of letters, accounts and invoices and may cause all testimony to be reduced to writing and preserved (§ 16). Any person who neglects or refuses to attend or answer becomes liable to a fine of one hundred dollars, and if he be the owner or importer the appraisement by the board will be final. False swearing before the board is perjury and subjects the goods of the perjurer to forfeiture. The decisions of the general appraisers are preserved and an abstract of the more important ones is published at least once a week.

It will be noticed that this remedy as to amounts and rates of duty, while not so narrow as that existing between 1839 and 1845, which was simply an administrative appeal to the Secretary of the Treasury,[1] is not so liberal as that existing between 1845 and 1890. For it now lies in the discretion of the court to refuse the importer any remedy except that of appeal to the Board of General Appraisers. As regards appraisement, the remedy provided by the administrative bill is more effectual, since the Board of General Appraisers is more worthy of confidence than the former board to which appeals as to appraisement went.

During the first three months after their appointment, the general appraisers decided 779 cases of appeals on questions of value, 713 of which were in New York. During the same period they received 1,700 protests upon questions of classification, of which 1,129 related to importations at New York. They disposed of 704 of these cases, leaving 996 pending. From this it would seem that if the appraisers are to do their work well and carefully an increase in the force is necessary; otherwise they will fall behind almost as rapidly as the courts have done.

---

[1] The Supreme Court decided that there was no judicial remedy. Cary *vs.* Curtis, 3 How. 236, see *supra*, p. 55.

4. Abolition of Damage Allowances.

For many years there had been complaints by collectors and special agents that excessive damage allowances were claimed by importers, and that the decision of these questions were of such extreme difficulty as to afford opportunity for considerable frauds upon the revenue. It was urged that the provisions of the old law (1799), allowing deductions for damage to goods on the voyage, were adopted at a time when long cruises in small sailing vessels furnished the only means of importation. At that time damage to imported goods was natural and probable, and the deduction of such loss was just and fair. But it was contended that under our changed methods of transportation damage was extremely improbable, and may in any case be amply insured against; that in the absence of knowledge as to the original condition of the goods the custom house officials are entirely unable to determine the existence or amount of damage. To meet these objections the decision is thrown upon the importer himself. The recent law provides that within ten days after entry the importer may abandon to the United States, without payment of duties, all or any portion of his goods above ten per cent. of the total quantity or value of the invoice. The goods so abandoned are then to be sold at public auction or otherwise disposed of to the credit of the United States.

5. Manufacturing in Bond and Drawbacks.

The Act of 1799, contained ten sections regulating the payment of drawbacks.[1] The main provisions were as follows:

The amount of duties paid on the articles exported was required to be at least fifty dollars. The goods were to be exported in the original packages, without diminution or change of the articles contained therein.[2] Forms were prescribed in

---

[1] The former laws made similar but less extensive provisions. Act of 1789, § 30, etc.

[2] The exporter of liquors or unrefined sugars was allowed, however, (§ 75) under supervision of an officer, to have the casks filled up or to use new casks where necessary.

which the exporter was to prove under oath that the duties had been paid, and to state their amount. Provision was made for the transportation of imported goods from one district to another, as well as for their exportation. Proof was required of the arrival of the goods at the foreign port and the forms therefor laid down.[1]

Subsequent laws repealed some of these provisions and made other slight changes. But the manner of establishing, determining and paying drawbacks has always been left largely to the regulation of the Secretary of the Treasury. Drawbacks were also allowed on the exportation of articles which had paid internal revenue taxes.

It is worth while to note a curious result of the system of drawbacks toward the end of the last century. The Act of June 5, 1794, imposed an internal revenue tax of eight cents a pound on all snuff manufactured in the United States, and to offset this tax increased the import duty on snuff to twelve cents a pound. On March 3, 1795, the internal tax was replaced by a tax on snuff mills, and a drawback of six cents a pound was allowed for all snuff exported. The result was that the drawback exceeded the tax, and that snuff now began to be manufactured in large quantities for the sake of the drawback. This necessarily led to the suspension and finally to the repeal of the law. But the system of drawbacks was continued in the case of other articles subject to internal taxation. The same system was renewed in connection with the internal revenue taxes levied during the war with England.

The great extension of the internal taxes during the civil war increased the importance of the drawback system.[2] The

[1] See *supra* pp. 27 and 31.

[2] Prior to 1842, in the exportation of goods on which the duty had not been paid, the debentures given to secure payment were cancelled on the payment of one per cent. of the amount, but on the adoption of cash payments there was naturally an immediate and heavy falling off in the amount of dutiable goods, *etc.* exported (see *supra* p. 50). Indeed, it was principally to restore this export business that the warehousing system was adopted, though it did not accomplish the

Act of August 5, 1861,[1] provided that on all goods manufactured wholly of imported materials[2] on which duties had been paid, a drawback equal to ninety per cent. of the duties so paid should be allowed under such regulations as the Secretary of the Treasury might appoint.

The recent tariff act provides (§ 25) that on the exportation of articles, in the manufacture of which imported materials are used, there shall be allowed a drawback equal to ninety-nine per cent. of the duties paid, provided that the articles be so made that the quantity or measure of the dutiable goods can be ascertained. The Secretary of the Treasury is empowered to make regulations by which the imported material in an exported product should be identified, the quantity used and the duties paid ascertained, the facts of the manufacture of the product in the United States and its export therefrom determined, and the drawback paid. To accomplish all this the Secretaries' regulations are of necessity so strict and burdensome that a great part of the contemplated benefit of the drawback is lost.

The early laws all allowed bounties on the exportation of pickled fish. The act of July 30, 1846 (§ 5), substituted in lieu of these bounties a drawback equal to the amount of the duties paid on the salt used in curing the fish, and the act of July 28, 1866,[3] provided that salt in bond might be used for that purpose and the duties remitted on the amount proved to have been so used. The use of materials in bond has been considerably extended by the recent act. It provides (§ 10) that all medicines, preparations, compositions, perfumery, cosmetics, cordials and other liquors manufactured wholly or

desired result, and the storage of goods to be re-exported has never been its chief function.

[1] 37th Congress, Session 1, Chapter 45.

[2] The law of June 6, 1872, Vol. 17, Statutes at Large, 238, extended this to certain classes of manufactured articles in which the imported material " exceeds one-half of the value of the material used."

[3] Re-enacted June 6, 1872.

in part of domestic spirits intended for exportation, may be thus manufactured in bond and exported under the inspection of appointed officers. A similar privilege was extended to smelters and refiners by section twenty-four. A temporary provision of like nature was made for the refining of sugar in bond without the payment of duty between March 1 and April 1, 1891.

6. Abolition of Fees.

By section twenty-two all fees exacted and oaths administered were abolished except in so far as they were provided for in the act itself. When such fees would formerly have constituted, in whole or in part, the salary of any officer, the law provided that such officer should receive a fixed sum for each year equal to the amount which he would have been entitled to receive as fees for such services during the year. Thus a step was taken towards the desired total abolition of fees. But the salaries of officers were left as indeterminate, as unclassified and as hopelessly disproportioned to their duties and responsibilities as ever. Another reform, the need of which has been long felt, but which this act, like its predecessors, did not attempt, and which for political reasons is distasteful to our legislators, is the abolition of many useless and expensive customs establishments and the consolidation of districts. This reform is demanded alike for reasons of economy and because of the changed conditions of commerce and transportation.

There are other reforms and experiments now demanded and advocated, and we may look forward to more or less frequent legislation on this subject. It is almost impossible to administer changing laws with an unchanged system. As long as the tariff policy of our government remains unsettled, we may expect its customs method to remain unfixed.

May we not say that from an administrative as well as an economic standpoint, perhaps as much mischief has resulted from the frequent changes in our tariff laws as from their defects?

CONCLUSION.

GENERAL TENDENCIES OF TARIFF ADMINISTRATION IN THE UNITED STATES.

FROM this brief outline of what seem to be the more prominent features of our tariff administration, we may say that there has been, on the whole, a steady development towards more stringent supervision, regulation and control over the importer. In summing up this development, perhaps we may roughly divide the objects of the system into three classes, conveniently designated as the protective, the preventive and the punitive.

I. *The Protective System.*—Under the early laws the protection of the revenue was insufficient because of long credits, *etc.* After long discussion and severe experience, the protection was made complete by the harsh requirement of cash payments, in 1842. The tendency from that time on was to alleviate the rigor of that law by more liberal provisions, such as warehousing and its accompaniments. During the civil war there was a sharp reaction and a curtailment of those privileges, followed ever since by their steady extension, without in any way endangering the revenue.

II. *The Preventive System.* Again we find the system starting with slight preventives against fraud, and apparently administered for the first quarter of a century upon the basis of confidence in the importer. When this confidence was once lost, it was lost never to return. Since then the laws of entry, inspection and appraisement have been steadily more extended, and have become increasingly severe.

III. *The Punitive System.* The law of 1799 contained heavy penalties and allowed summary methods of procedure.

(88)

These methods were rarely resorted to, however, although suits increased gradually as time went on. The rigorous enforcement of the harsh provisions of the law of 1861 brought about their extensive modification, until they were practically abolished in 1874. This over-action has been followed by the moderate reaction of the last law, whose adoption has been too recent to allow even of prediction as to future enactments.

www.ingramcontent.com/pod-product-compliance
Lightning Source LLC
Chambersburg PA
CBHW030028290326
41934CB00005B/529

9 781616 190903